Inspiring Stories
For 9 Year Old Kids

Tales That Educate, Entertain, and Empower Young Readers

Hayden Fox

© **Copyright - All rights reserved.**

The content contained within this book may not be reproduced, duplicated or transmitted without direct written permission from the author or the publisher.

Under no circumstances will any blame or legal responsibility be held against the publisher, or author, for any damages, reparation, or monetary loss due to the information contained within this book, either directly or indirectly.

Legal Notice:

This book is copyright protected. It is only for personal use. You cannot amend, distribute, sell, use, quote or paraphrase any part, or the content within this book, without the consent of the author or publisher.

Disclaimer Notice:

Please note the information contained within this document is for educational and entertainment purposes only. All effort has been executed to present accurate, up to date, reliable, complete information. No warranties of any kind are declared or implied. Readers acknowledge that the author is not engaged in the rendering of legal, financial, medical or professional advice. The content within this book has been derived from various sources. Please consult a licensed professional before attempting any techniques outlined in this book.

By reading this document, the reader agrees that under no circumstances is the author responsible for any losses, direct or indirect, that are incurred as a result of the use of the information contained within this document, including, but not limited to, errors, omissions, or inaccuracies.

Table of Contents

A MAGICAL CAST OF CREATURES 6

A LAND OF INSPIRATION (THE AUTHOR'S NOTE) 8

ENCHANTED MUSHROOM SOUP 9

GIANT ADVICE 25

THE DRAGON WITHOUT A NAME 40

PIE AND OTHER MAGICAL DISASTERS 54

FRANKLIN THE FAIRY TAKES A VERY BIG JOB 68

A COIN FOR A WISH 77

THE MAGICAL MEETUP MYSTERY 91

A Magical Cast of Creatures

Bobbles the Goblin: A very tiny and very brave hero.

Bangles the Goblin: Bobbles' brother, not as tiny or as brave.

??? the Goblin: Bobbles' other brother, who had his name stolen by fairies.

Jammy the Troll: Big and Strong and Hairy and just trying his best.

??? the Green Dragon: A giant monster who can't remember his name, thanks to the fairies. (These fairies are out of control.)

Naron the Giant: Holds up the world. It is *very* heavy.

Whimsy the Wizard: Not actually a wizard. Has a magic wand and tries really hard, though.

Grandma Wist: Left her magic wand with her grandson. That may have been a mistake.

Bitey the Cat: A regular cat. Learned to talk to make her owner happy.

Became mayor of Dewdrop Hill.

The Wandering Knights: A band of knights in search of treasure. One is riding a pig.

Stormblast Thunderfist: A little boy who misses his friend. Chose his own name and did an amazing job.

Katey the Kitsune: A magic fox with nine tails. Has a job as a detective when Dewdrop Hill needs one, which is not very often.

Franklin: A young fairy who isn't very good at actually being a fairy. He's good at something; he just isn't sure what.

Ana: Queen of the fairies. (What is she doing with all those extra names?)

A Land of Inspiration (The Author's Note)

The village of Dewdrop Hill, and the area around it, is full of people who are trying their best. They try to be honest, brave, and generous. They are curious, thoughtful, and they never give up. They are kind to others, creative, and ready to try things in new ways when something doesn't work out.

Sometimes they do a great job, and sometimes they fail even though they tried. That's okay, though, because the people in Dewdrop Hill know that failure is part of life and with a little luck they'll get a chance to try again and make things right. They know if they keep trying their best, everyone in Dewdrop Hill will have a happy life.

I hope that when you read these stories about Dewdrop Hill, you see how hard the people who live there try and their stories inspire you to try, too.

And the stories are really fun, so I hope you have fun reading them.

Enchanted Mushroom Soup

Goblins love most things. Every goblin loves different things, but they are a happy, curious bunch, so no matter what it is, chances are good that there is a goblin who loves it.

Three goblin brothers found themselves in the forest one day because they were hungry, and their favorite things were exploring, green tree leaves, and mushroom soup. They couldn't have mushroom soup without mushrooms, and so they went exploring to find some.

All goblins are small, but the youngest brother, Bobbles, was small even for a goblin, so he stayed in the back. His middle brother Bangles was a regular size for a goblin, so he walked in the middle. And his oldest brother Larry was big for a goblin, so he led the way.

They must have been having a lucky day, because the mushrooms were easy to find. Big, fat, beautiful mushrooms, all in a neat circle. Perfect for soup.

The goblins jumped up and down in excitement, because even though mushrooms were ordinary, they were the brothers' favorite thing and that made them exciting.

An excited goblin is not a careful goblin, and while Larry was jumping up and down, he fell into the circle of mushrooms... and disappeared.

"Larry, where did you go?" Bangles cried.

Bangles jumped into the circle to look for Larry, but as soon as he did, he disappeared too.

Since Bobbles was smaller than most goblins, he was also more cautious. He looked carefully at the mushrooms and saw tiny pink sparkles like glitter on them. All mushrooms were exciting, but these mushrooms were more exciting than most. They were enchanted fairy mushrooms.

Goblins needed to be wise to grow old, and Bobbles had been told by very old, very wise goblins to never disturb a circle of enchanted fairy mushrooms. But he didn't know what to do without his brothers, and so Bobbles stepped inside the circle and disappeared too.

The good news was that Bobbles found Bangles and Larry right away. The bad news was that they had entered the fairy kingdom, without an invitation to boot, and could not see any way out.

The sky was yellow and the clouds were pink, like floating cotton candy. The tree trunks were golden and the leaves on the golden trees were a shiny blue. The fairy kingdom was very strange, Bobbles thought, but also very beautiful.

The fairies came to see them immediately. The goblins were not used to seeing creatures smaller than they were, but the fairies were not much larger than one of the goblins' hands. They had shimmering wings that the goblins could see right through and hair in playful, bouncing curls. But they looked very serious and stern-faced. Each of them carried a spear as sharp as a bee's stinger and just as painful, if they decided to use them.

One of the fairies, who looked more noble than the others, said, "This is the fairy kingdom. You are not fairies. You are trespassing. Explain yourselves."

Larry, being the oldest and the biggest, stepped forward to answer. "We are very sorry. We were hungry, and so we were looking for mushrooms for our mushroom soup. We found a ring of mushrooms, but we didn't know they belonged to you."

The fairies began speaking to each other rapidly in words the goblins did not understand. But the fairy who had spoken to the brothers waved her hand and they stopped.

"Very understandable," the fairy said. "My name is Ana, and I am queen of the fairies. May I have your name?"

"Of course! My name is Larry."

"Thank you for your gift," Queen Ana said. "In return, would you like to join us for a feast?"

Bobbles looked at Bangles and his other brother. He wasn't sure it was a good idea, but his brothers were already following the fairies, led by their hungry stomachs. He didn't know how to get home and he didn't want to leave his brothers, so he followed them.

The fairies' banquet hall was beautiful, with a roof made of leaves and walls of gleaming polished stone—a single stone the fairies had turned into a great hall with their magic. But, although it was amazing to look at, it was not goblin-sized; it was fairy-sized.

Ana looked at the goblins, who looked positively giant next to the fairy village. "Oh, I'm afraid that will just not do. I'm casting a spell, so hold on to your shoes."

Before Bobbles could react, shimmering sparkles surrounded him, Bangles, and his other brother. He did not feel himself shrink, but one moment he was goblin-sized and the next he was fairy-sized. Every leaf was as big as a blanket, and the trees were so tall he couldn't see the tops. But everything in the fairy village was now the proper size, and he could smell the delicious food inside the great hall. He tried not to look directly at the fairies, who now seemed strong and imposing, especially with their bee-stinger spears. Bangles and his other brother were already headed inside, so Bobbles followed them.

The inside of the great hall was even more beautiful than the outside. Long tables filled with food got his attention first, but when Bobbles looked up, he saw the ceiling was painted. Half showed a beautiful noon sky with pink clouds and red sun, and the other half showed a night sky with a large glowing moon and countless stars. Bobbles thought he could see the stars twinkling and the sun shining. It was fairy magic on full display, making the great hall feel like an outdoor picnic and both day and night at once.

Bobbles watched his brothers rush over to a table to look at the food. With their new fairy-like size, there were single cherries that looked as big as pumpkins, roasted onions bigger than any roast Bobbles had ever seen, and giant tomatoes sliced into steaks. But what they noticed most happily were the big bowls of enchanted mushroom soup.

There was just one problem: no chairs. Other fairies sat in chairs, but each had their own and there were no extras. The fairy queen was a good host, however, and so when she saw them, she waved her hand and her fairy magic made chairs for them to sit in.

"Here you go," Queen Ana said. "Aren't they the finest chairs you've ever seen?"

Bangles sat in his chair. It was hard and uncomfortable, but he was so happy to be eating that he said, "Oh, yes, certainly. This is the finest chair there ever was."

Bobbles' other brother sat in his chair. It was too soft, very lumpy, and difficult to sit in. But he was happy to be eating, too, so he said, "Oh, yes, I agree. This is the finest chair there ever was."

Bobbles sat in his chair, which was crooked and had a wobble because the legs weren't quite right. He didn't want to be mean, but he didn't want to lie either, so he said, "Thank you for this chair. You have been a good host."

Queen Ana studied them carefully and then smiled. "This is the fairy feast, which has been here as long as there have been fairies. Any fairy can eat here, any time, with great joy and no cost."

Bangles and the other brother started eating, their manners forgotten as they tasted the magic food. The cherries were the sweetest they had ever tasted, and their mouths became red with cherry juice. The onions were soft and delicious, better than any they had ever roasted. And the enchanted mushroom soup was so good, so tasty, so amazing, that they thought they would stay forever and eat soup under the magic sunlight for the rest of their days.

The food was very tempting, but Bobbles hesitated. He saw the way his brothers ate so quickly, and he was worried. Queen Ana looked at them with a smile, but Bobbles wanted to ask her more questions.

"Excuse me, Queen Ana," Bobbles said. "You said this food was for fairies and that fairies could eat here any time without cost, but I am not a fairy. I am a goblin."

"That is true," Queen Ana said.

"Is there a cost to eating here, for people who are not fairies?" Bobbles asked.

"Those who begin to eat may have as much as they like," Queen Ana said.

Bobbles suspected he should choose his words very carefully.

"Your food all looks so very delicious. May I and my brothers eat from your feast without a cost?"

"You are welcome to the feast," the fairy queen said. "But nothing from the fairy kingdom can leave it. We once had a beautiful jewel that brought joy to every fairy who looked at it, but it was taken, so now, we don't let anything else leave. But please, enjoy."

The fairy queen left Bobbles alone so she could go and talk with other guests. Bobbles watched Bangles and their other brother eat bowl after bowl of the enchanted mushroom soup until they fell asleep. Bobbles was very hungry and very jealous, but he did not eat the soup because he thought the fairy queen was being tricky with her words. Even though she wasn't lying, he thought that she wasn't exactly telling the truth, either.

Queen Ana returned later, after most of the fairies had eaten and gone home. Bangles and the other brother were still fast asleep, right at the table.

"Did you enjoy the feast?" Queen Ana asked Bobbles.

"I had a wonderful time," Bobbles said. "But I did not eat the food. My brothers and I can't stay here, and I didn't want to carry your food away inside me."

"How respectful," Queen Ana said. "Unfortunately, your brothers did eat our feast, so I'm afraid they will have to stay."

"I need Bangles and—" Bobbles paused, thinking. He knew he had two brothers, but he could only remember one of their names. "I need my brothers to come with me. I don't think I'm feeling well, I can't remember his name." He nodded to his oldest brother.

"Oh, that name?" Queen Ana said. "You don't need to worry about that name. He gave it to me, and I will keep it safe. They will be safe here too. Are you sure you wouldn't like to stay here with them?"

Bobbles was getting worried. "I would like to stay with my brothers. I want to be polite, but I need them to come with me. Is there anything I can offer to trade for them?"

The fairy queen got a look in her eye that was maybe not quite evil, but cunning and clever. "Are you a brave goblin?"

"I try my best to be brave, but I am not always brave, because I am so small. Now I am even smaller, which I admit is rather interesting."

Queen Ana nodded. "When I asked about the chair, you were polite and honest, even though it wasn't the best chair. When I offered you the feast, you were polite and honest and didn't take without asking. When I asked if you were brave you admitted you were not. You are a very polite and honest goblin, and that makes me think I can trust you."

"Thank you, your majesty," Bobbles said.

"Because you are honest, I will trust you with an important job. If you do it for me, I will return your brothers." Queen Ana waved her hand. Bangles and the other brother disappeared. "For now, I'll put them to bed and let them sleep happily. Will you do the job for me?"

Bobbles put a finger in his ear and scratched. "I think I should hear about the job before I answer," he said.

"Polite, honest, brave-but-not-brave, and smart as well," Queen Ana said. "Impressive. There is a large and powerful dragon in a cave. It is not in the fairy kingdom, so I don't think a fairy should go there. The dragon has the jewel that I mentioned a moment ago. It's called The Ear of the Fairy Queen, because when I have it, I can hear everything in the land. If you get that jewel for me, I will trade it for your brothers."

Bobbles did not like scary things, and a powerful dragon sounded quite scary. But he would try to be brave to save his brothers. Since honesty was a good thing when talking to fairy queens and most other creatures, perhaps it would be good for talking with dragons, too.

"Will you get me my prize jewel, honest goblin?" asked the fairy queen.

"I will go see this dragon, and I will not return empty-handed," Bobbles said.

His adventure was just beginning, and when it was over he would be treating himself to some regular mushroom soup.

Giant Advice

Jammy the troll sat alone under his bridge, and he was very grumpy. He met people from time to time when they crossed his bridge, but no one ever stayed or even asked his name. He was big and strong and did a very good job guarding the bridge, keeping it safe, and repairing it when a stone fell off or the moss grew over it too much. Still, no one noticed.

Jammy decided that he would find someone even bigger and stronger than he was and ask for their advice. If Jammy could become the biggest and strongest troll there ever was, surely people would have to notice him.

One day, a traveler came to use his bridge, but the traveler was not big or strong at all. It was a frail old woman, looking very weary as she leaned heavily on her walking stick. But she had an intelligent gleam in her eye, so Jammy decided he would ask for her help.

He asked the woman to pay the toll, and then asked her, "Ancient one, who is the biggest, strongest person you know of?"

The woman thought for a moment. "You are very big, Mr. Troll, which is why I paid the toll. I have met many creatures in my journeys, but I suppose the biggest and strongest person anywhere must be the giant holding up the world."

A giant holding up the world! Jammy couldn't imagine such a thing. What was the giant standing on, if it was carrying everything? It was a mystery that would have to wait. He cleaned up the bridge and made sure it was extra tidy. He wanted to leave a sign so travelers knew to pay the toll, but he wasn't very good at reading and writing yet, so he decided not to. He bundled up some bread and cheese and went in search of the giant holding up the world.

It was hard, and Jammy was discouraged. He tried to ask for help, but he was not very good at asking and the people he asked would usually run away screaming. Sometimes he didn't even get to ask a question before they ran! At least the little goblin had been helpful. Another time, he would have to practice being more gentle so people were not afraid of him.

He traveled through fields, and forests, and mountains. He crossed rivers, and swam through lakes, and splashed through swamps. He saw many amazing and wonderful things, but the thing that surprised him most of all was that other bridges did not seem to have trolls guarding them. How did they stay in good condition with no one to fix them up? He wanted to stay and fix them all, but first, he had to find the giant holding up the world.

Finally, Jammy came to a vast desert. He could not see the other side. In the distance, there was a dusty brown mountain blocking the way. Blocking the way for most things, he supposed, but he was a big and strong troll, and a very good climber. And so, he went on.

The desert was dry and hot and lonely, but it made Jammy happy to explore somewhere new—except for the lonely part, anyway. But if he could meet the giant holding up the world, he would learn the secret of being big and strong, and then everyone would love him and he wouldn't be lonely anymore. Then, he could tell his new friends about his adventures.

When Jammy reached the mountain, he discovered it was very strange. It wasn't like the other mountains he had crossed at all. The surface was brown and rough like leather, smooth in parts, but with deep grooves. He imagined most creatures would have a very difficult time climbing the strange mountain, but Jammy was a very good climber. And so, he went on.

He climbed and climbed until he reached the top. He could see all the lands he had traveled across. Desert. Forests. Swamps. He could even see the village of Dewdrop Hill, which he hoped to visit someday.

It was hard to stand on the top of the mountain. The surface was smooth and clear and a little bit slippery. The top of the mountain was also flat, which Jammy found very surprising. Weren't mountains pointy at the top? Then, Jammy realized he had made a mistake. He wasn't standing on top of a mountain. He was standing on a fingernail. In fact, he was standing atop a very, very, very big finger.

He walked along the fingernail until it disappeared, making way for more of the brown leathery stuff Jammy now realized was skin. He walked for hours and hours, occasionally passing giant hairs taller than he was and thick enough he would need an axe to cut one. That might be a prize all by itself, if someone needed a giant's hair, but Jammy needed to press on if he wanted the secret to being big and strong.

He made it past the hand, up the arm to the elbow, and then up the elbow to the shoulder. Sometimes he could walk, and sometimes he had to climb.

He was very tired, but he would not give up.

When he finally made it to the giant's shoulder, he was amazed by what he saw. Far below him he could see the entire world, cradled carefully in the giant's hands. And above him was the giant's face.

The giant's eyes were closed, and he looked older than anyone Jammy had ever seen. He had long white hair that fell down his back and so many wrinkles on his face Jammy could barely make out his features, except a thin line of a mouth and a giant giant's nose, which was also filled with long white hair.

Jammy didn't want to startle the giant, because if the giant jumped in surprise it could be very bad news. But the giant didn't notice him and he didn't know what else to do, so he called out.

"Great and mighty giant, can you hear me?" Jammy yelled.

One eye opened slowly, green as an emerald. The giant turned his head carefully, to look at his shoulder.

"I can hear you," the giant said with a low voice that sounded like thunder and earthquakes. "But I think you may be lost. No one has ever climbed onto me to come see me before, and it seems rather impolite to climb on someone to talk to them."

"Would you have heard me if I didn't? From all the way down there?" asked Jammy.

The giant let out a sigh. "I suppose not. Where are you from? The rock? That can't be."

"It is," said Jammy. "I've come a very long way. I'm Jammy."

The giant's other eye opened now, in a look Jammy thought was surprise. The giant looked down at the world and said, "I was just carrying this stone because I liked it. Who knew there were things living on it? I suppose I will have to be more careful with it from now on. My name is Naron, although no one has asked my name in a very long time."

"No one notices me, Naron," Jammy said. "I try to be big and strong and work very hard, but no one notices me. How can I be bigger and stronger so other people will like me?"

The giant laughed. His shoulders shook, and Jammy had to throw himself down and hang on with all his might just so he didn't fall off. When Naron noticed, he tried to stop laughing, but it took a long time.

"Did you come and ask me because I am so big and strong?" Naron asked.

"Yes," Jammy said.

"Look around, new friend," Naron said. "No one notices me, either."

Jammy looked around. The sky was everywhere around them, with bright, beautiful stars. The universe was so large that looking at it made Jammy feel dizzy. From way up here, it was just him and Naron. Maybe the giant was lonely, just like him.

"I hoped you would have a secret to share, so I could feel stronger and more valuable," Jammy said. He was disappointed.

"Why, you are the first person to ever visit me," the giant said. "I suppose a wizard spoke with me once, but they used a magic spell to talk with me. They didn't come to visit. No one else could possibly travel across this entire stone and then all the way up my body, unless they were your size. Doesn't that make you the strongest in all your land?"

"I guess," Jammy said. It did not make him feel better. Had he really traveled all this way for nothing? He thought about having to climb back down and then walk all the way home, knowing the whole time that he had failed.

Naron felt bad for his new friend. He knew Jammy was feeling sad and hoping Naron would make him feel better. But since no one came to visit Naron, he didn't feel like he was very good at helping, either. Maybe everyone felt that way sometimes, no matter how big and strong they were.

"I will tell you my secret," Naron said. "Perhaps it can be our secret, together. Although I wish more people understood it, so maybe we should tell people, and not let it be a secret at all."

Jammy looked up at the giant. Naron's face was framed with stars.

"It doesn't matter how big and strong you are," Naron said. "Sometimes you will feel good about yourself, and sometimes you won't. But the most important thing to remember is that you know yourself best of all. You know you are trying very hard, and you know the things you like to do. You know the things you are good at, and the things you aren't good at yet that you will practice. Other people don't know you as well as you do, so if you decide you're doing great at being yourself, then you are."

"I don't know about that," Jammy said. "It feels too easy."

The giant laughed again, although this time he tried not to laugh very hard.

"It's not easy at all," Naron said. "Especially on days when you're not feeling very good about yourself. But it's okay if some days are hard. You're still doing great at being you."

"But how do you know that's true?" Jammy asked. "Especially on the days when you're feeling lonely."

"Look at me," Naron said. "I'm holding the whole rock where you live, and I didn't even know it was an important rock. I didn't even know I was doing a good job, but I was. That happens sometimes, too. I think as long as you care about people and things and do your best to take care of them, then you're doing better than you think. Do you take care of things, Jammy?"

"I take care of bridges, because I'm a troll," Jammy said.

Naron wrinkled his nose. He didn't know what a "bridge" was, exactly, but he was glad it was important to Jammy.

"See?" Naron said. "You're doing so much better than you thought. Even if people don't know you're helping them, you're still helping. Just like me."

Naron closed his eyes, and after a few minutes Jammy realized the old giant was sleeping. Jammy sat on the giant's shoulder for a long time, looking at the stars and thinking about what he had learned. Even if other people didn't know how hard he was trying, he did. And that was important.

"Thank you!" Jammy called out to his new friend Naron. "I think I should probably go home now, and make sure all the bridges are okay."

The giant's eyes opened again, and he gave Jammy a big smile. "Would you like me to set you down on the rock?" he asked. "I know you are big and strong enough to climb back on your own, but if I could tell you another secret, it's okay to ask for help when you need it." Naron winked.

"Yes, please," Jammy said. "It was a very, very, very long walk."

The giant carefully held out a hand, and Jammy climbed on, ready to be home again. He wondered, just for a moment, what exactly his friend Naron was standing on. Then he decided he would rather be fixing bridges, and he would save that adventure for another time.

The Dragon Without a Name

The forest was dark, and it did not look friendly. It looked like it was full of spiders and wolves and creepy creatures. Bobbles had never gone to the forest before, and now he had to go all by himself. He had never been without his brothers before, and now he was alone.

The fairy circle he had come from was gone, and there was nowhere else to go. He would have to be brave and go into the forest, because it was the right thing to do and because he had no other choice.

"I wish this dragon lived in a nice field," Bobbles thought. "Actually, I wish there wasn't a dragon at all." Treasure laying around with no one guarding it. What a nice world that would be.

Bobbles didn't walk far before he was completely lost. No sun came through the thick leaves, and it was impossible to see more than a few feet through the trees. But there was only one path, so he followed it. If there was one thing Bobbles had learned, it was that trusting fairies was a bad idea, but he had no choice.

The trail continued. Bobbles was sure something would jump out of the forest at any moment to eat him, and he did NOT want to be eaten. But the fairy queen had told him not to return empty-handed, and there was no one else who could go with him, so he continued.

The forest path led him on. It was scary, and his heart was pounding even though he hadn't come to any harm so far. After walking for a long time, Bobbles saw the entrance to a cave. It was barely big enough for him to slip through, and certainly not big enough for a dragon to enter. The dragon must get in another way, but Bobbles felt lucky he did not need to find the main entrance. He slipped into the dark cave.

Bobbles wished he had brought a torch. Before long, it was so dark he couldn't see at all. Normally he wasn't afraid of the dark, but most dark didn't have dragons in it. He pushed on, feeling along the walls with his fingers. Up ahead, he could see a faint glow. He didn't know if that was the right place, but it was the only light he could see, so he went towards it.

Then, Bobbles tripped. The sound echoed through the cave. A dragon roared.

"Come out, little creature," the dragon said. "Come out and I won't eat you.

But if I have to look for you it will make me very hungry."

Bobbles shook all over. He was so scared. He wanted his brothers back. He wanted to run away and hide. He did not want to be eaten, especially not by something with such sharp teeth and hot breath. But he believed the dragon and knew he couldn't see his brothers again without the dragon's treasure. He wanted to run away and hide. Instead, he stood up, brushed himself off, and stepped out to face the monster.

The cave opened into a large cavern, so big Bobbles could barely see the end of it. Above him, he could see the sky. The dragon must get out by flying, he thought.

The dragon. Bobbles felt his heart race. It was huge and green, with a giant body, even bigger wings, and a long tail filled with spikes.

The dragon's very powerful and very long neck turned toward Bobbles, and the dragon lowered its head down toward the goblin. The dragon's breath was hot and dangerous, and above all it did not smell very good.

The dragon laughed. Small jets of fire shot out of its nostrils along with a steady stream of smoke. Bobbles jumped aside with a yell and slapped out a small fire that had started on his pant leg. He wasn't hurt, but he thought he would smell like smoke for a long time.

"Of all the little creatures who come to visit me, you are the littlest!" the dragon said, delighted.

Maybe that was good luck. Would the dragon leave him alone if he was too little to make a good snack?

"Look at you shake, little creature," the dragon said. Smoke still came out of his nose and his mouth. "I suppose if I was so little, I would be afraid of a lot of things too. Especially big, strong, dragons full of majesty."

The dragon spread its wings as far as it could, and it really was majestic. Its green scales glowed in the firelight, and its muscles rippled when it moved its huge body. If it decided to eat him, Bobbles had no hope. But he was getting that treasure.

"Dragon, sir?" Bobbles called out. He tried to make his voice sound big even though he wasn't. It sounded big to him, but he thought maybe it would still sound small to a dragon. "Or dragon, ma'am? Your Dragon Majesty?"

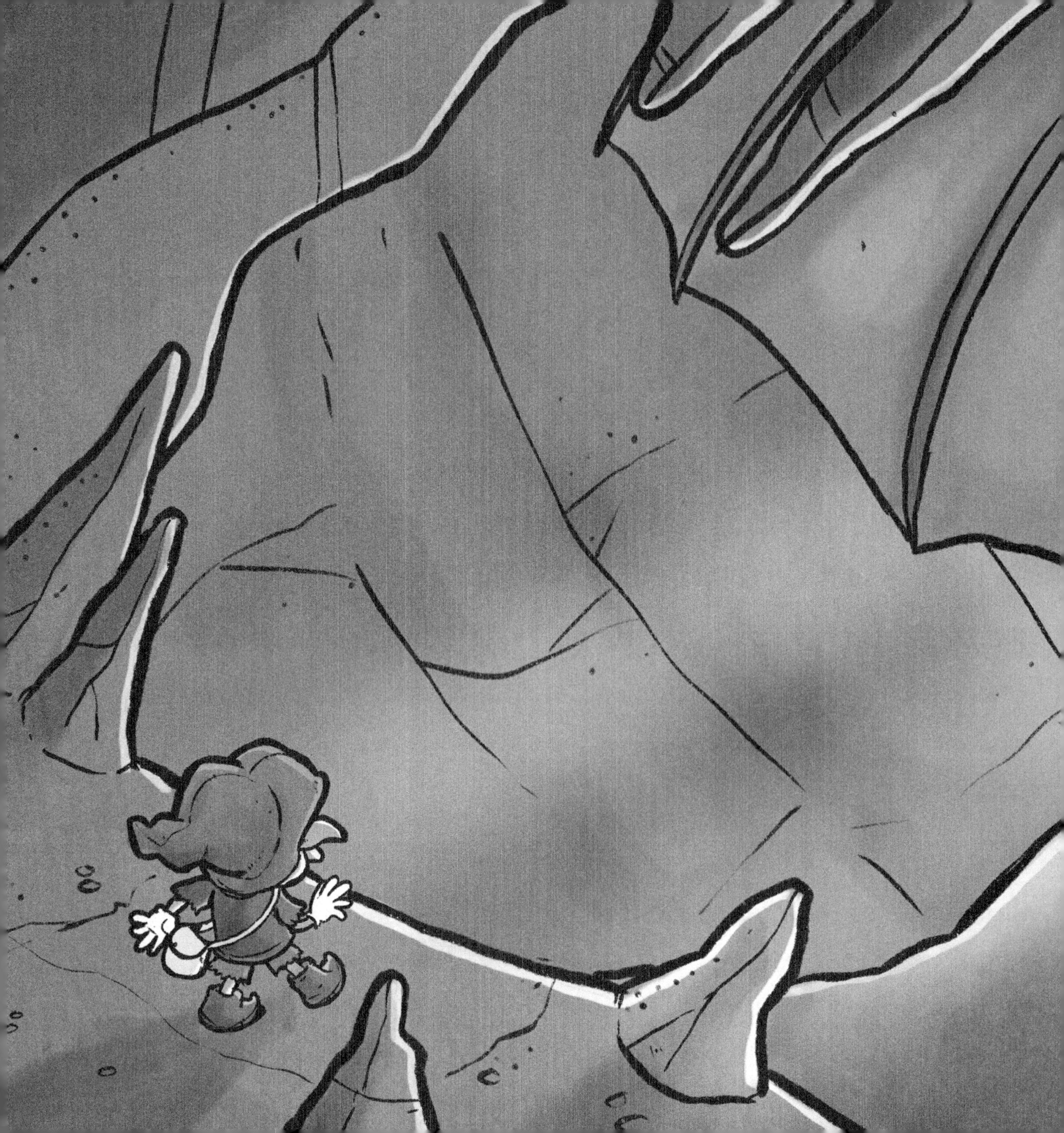

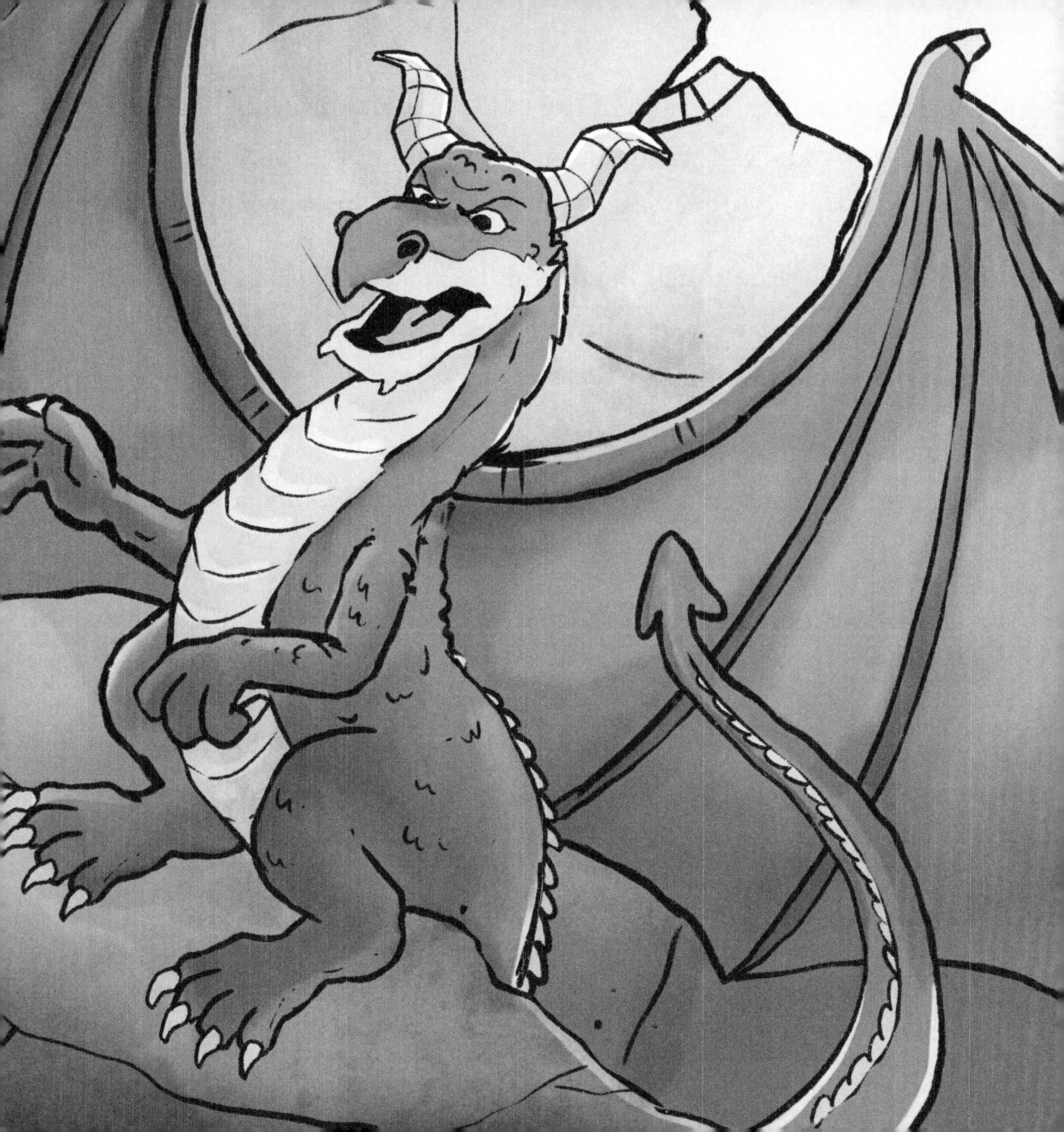

The dragon snorted, and a jet of fire lit the cave and turned a wall black. "I'm afraid I don't know. Fairies took my name, and now I cannot remember it." His eyes narrowed suspiciously. "Are you a fairy, little creature?"

Bobbles didn't want to tell the dragon he knew the fairies, but if there was one thing dealing with the fairies had taught him, it was that hiding the truth was a very bad idea.

"I am not a fairy, your dragon majesty! I would never steal your name. But the fairies did send me to your cave, I'm afraid," Bubbles admitted.

The dragon roared. The cave shook. Dust and small rocks rained from the ceiling. Bobbles coughed. All the dust made it hard to see, and his ears hurt from the dragon's mighty roar.

"I am going to eat you now," the dragon said. "Even though you are too tiny to be a good snack. The last time I talked to a fairy, they stole my name."

"Wait, wait, wait!" Bobbles yelled. "I said I'm not a fairy! My words can't trick you!"

The dragon looked thoughtful, even if he was still angry. "I suppose that I am very strong and you are a very weak little creature. You can tell me why you are here. Then I will eat you."

Bobbles did feel very small and very weak. Anyone would, in his situation. He was scared, and even worse, he was about to be eaten. But he had to keep trying if he had any hope of saving his brothers.

"The fairies want me to steal treasure from you in exchange for my brothers. They stole one of my brother's names too," he explained.

The dragon roared again. "No one steals from me!"

"I wouldn't dare, your dragon majesty. I knew I couldn't stand up to your, uh, majesty-ness."

"What sort of little creature are you?" the dragon asked. "A bug? Are bugs best eaten raw, or cooked?" The dragon looked at Bobbles curiously.

"I'm a goblin, your majesty-ness. And I don't think we're best eaten raw or cooked. I don't think goblins should be eaten at all," replied Bobbles.

"Sounds like something a snack would say," the dragon said.

Bobbles knew this might be his last chance. But he was going to be brave. "The fairies want the jewel they called the Ear of the Fairy Queen. It's blue and green and glows even with no light around."

"The Ear..." the dragon appeared to be thinking. "This ugly thing?"

The dragon plunged a claw into his pile of treasure and dug around for a long time. Bobbles could tell he was getting annoyed that he was unable to find the tiny jewel in the hoard. It would be a great time for Bobbles to sneak away, if he wanted to. He could walk away and be safe, and it was very tempting. But then he would never see his brothers again.

Finally the dragon pulled the jewel from the pile. It looked tiny, pinched between his giant claws on the other side of the cave. Bobbles would not have seen it at all except for the blue-green glow.

"I don't even want this thing!" The dragon roared with laughter. "I have to bury it deep in my hoard just so the light doesn't keep me awake when I try to sleep. I've been meaning to throw it away, but it's hard to keep things clean when you have so much." His mood suddenly soured. "But I don't know if I want to give it to a fairy, or to a goblin who comes from fairies.

Perhaps I will still eat you, and throw this thing in a lake."

Everything in Bobbles' mind told him to beg not to be eaten, or to run away and hide. But he was a clever goblin, and maybe there was a better way if he had the courage.

"Wait, your dragon majesty!" Bobbles yelled, trying to make his little voice sound big. "The fairies took your name, right? Keep the jewel with you. I will go back to the fairies and tell them you will trade The Ear of The Fairy Queen for your name. Then you can have your name back, and be rid of the jewel at the same time."

The dragon thought for a long time, perhaps wondering if this was a trick. Bobbles hoped that his honesty and bravery would help the dragon believe him.

"I don't even know how long my name has been forgotten," the dragon finally said sadly. "It feels as though it has always been forgotten, and I am always about to remember. I would like it back very much."

"It's a deal, then!" Bobbles cheered. "I would rather be a messenger for a dragon than a fairy, anyway." But Bobbles was still thinking. "The fairies said I couldn't return to them empty-handed. Do you suppose I could have some of your treasure, to meet that part of my promise?"

The dragon growled. "Greedy goblin," he accused.

"No, no, no," Bobbles promised. "Not any valuable treasure. Just the... regular kind? Something small, and not very special."

"If it wasn't special, I wouldn't keep it," the dragon said. "It's all special."

Still, the dragon dug around in his treasure some more until he found an empty chest. It looked tiny when the dragon was holding it, but quite large when he dropped it in front of Bobbles. Then the dragon scooped up a large pile of treasure and carefully picked out all the gold and jewels, keeping them to himself. He dumped a large pile of copper and silver coins over the chest and over Bobbles. Bobbles covered his head with his hands as the coins rained down, but soon the chest was full.

"Thank you, your majesty-ness," Bobbles said.

"Return to the fairies," the dragon said. "Tell them they can have their jewel when I can have my name."

"Yes, your majesty-ness," Bobbles said. He closed the treasure chest and lifted it. Luckily for him, goblins are strong even though they are small. It was still hard to lift, but he could do it. His bravery had paid off, and now he could return to the fairies with the treasure, save his brothers, and help the dragon, too.

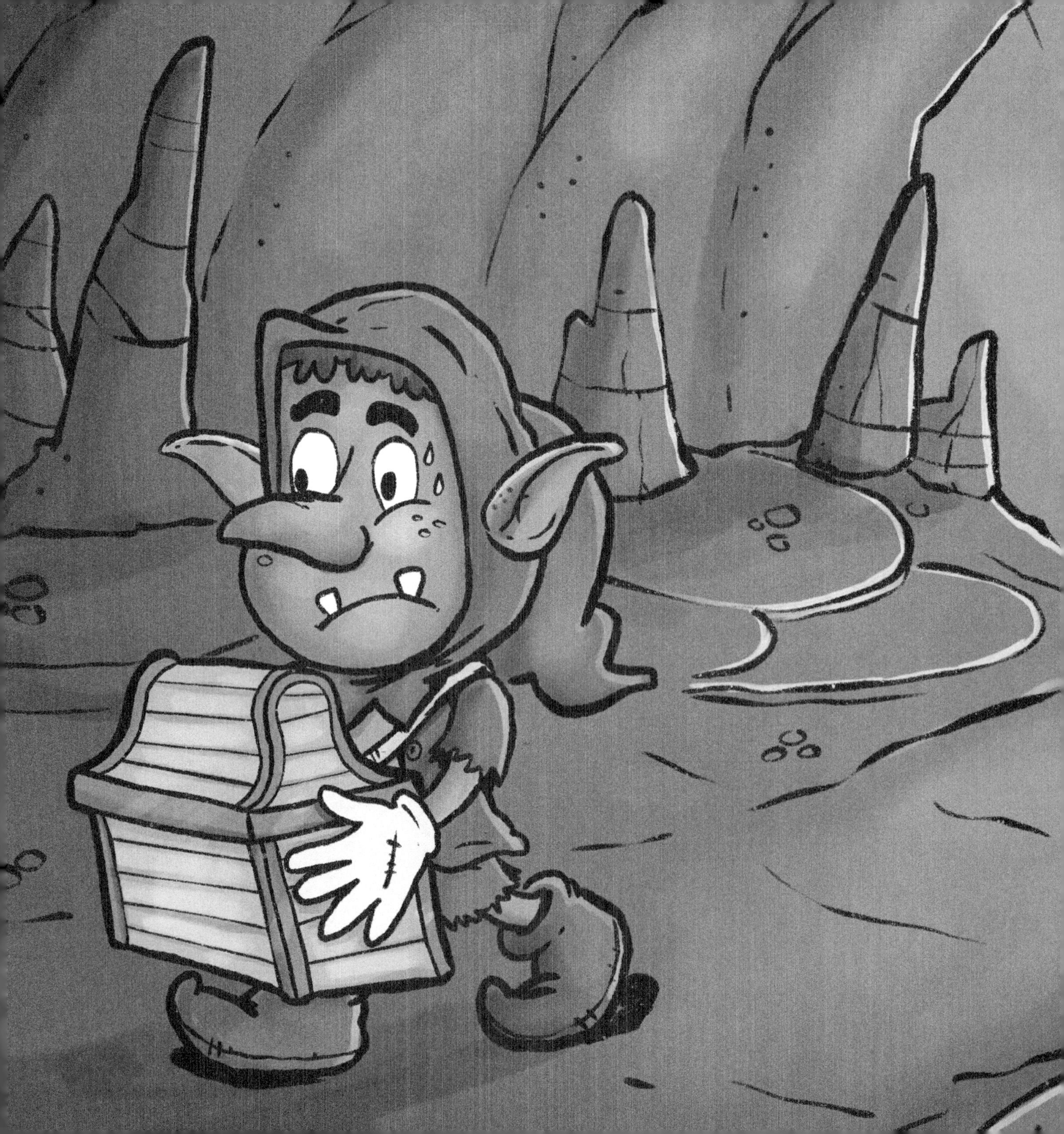

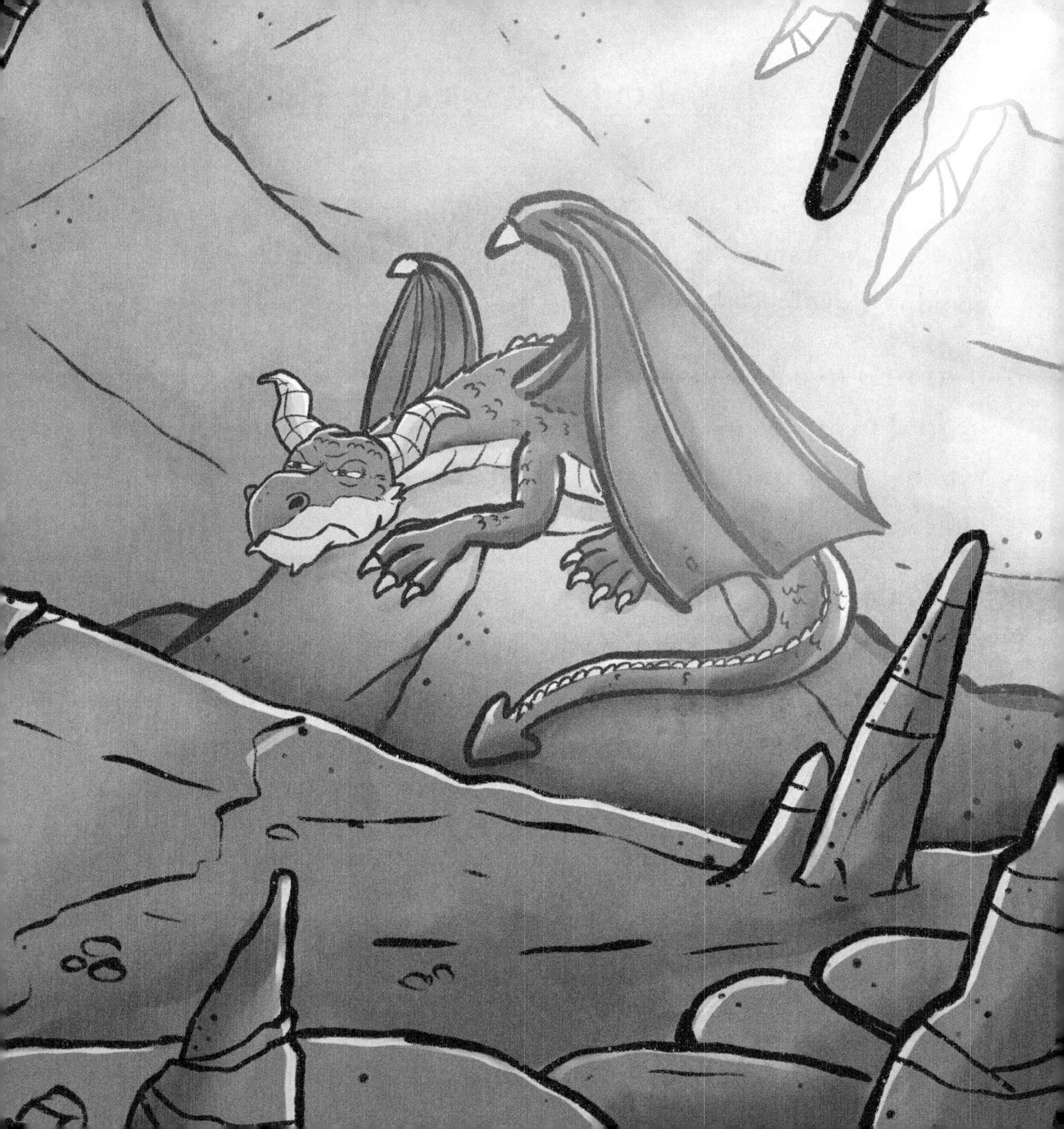

Pie and Other Magical Disasters

Whimsy the Wizard loved three things: oranges, pie, and magic. More than anything he wanted to try an orange pie, but no matter what he did, he couldn't make it work.

If he tried to put the oranges in the pie, it would be too wet and soggy. If he tried to dry the oranges, they got all chewy and then burned. He tried it with butter, he tried it with cream, he tried it with sugar, but he could never quite get it right.

But Whimsy the Wizard loved magic, so maybe he could use his magic wand to help. It wasn't his wand exactly, and he wasn't exactly supposed to be using it either, but his grandmother had been a very powerful wizardess and when she left the wand behind, Whimsy kept it as a special treasure.

Whimsy thought the wand was a toy, but one day, while he was holding the wand, he said, "I wish I had a piece of buttered toast, it's the thing I want the most." The wand glowed and sparked and created a delicious, crispy, perfect piece of buttered toast.

The orange pie was much trickier.

He rolled up the sleeves on his blue wizard robe and took the wand in his hand. "Pretty please make an orange pie, it's the thing I'd love to try!" he said.

The wand sparkled and glowed, let out a loud "pop," and created a delicious-looking pumpkin pie. Whimsy was confused. Pumpkin made great pies, but it wasn't the pie he wanted. Why didn't it give him an orange pie? Then he realized: Pumpkin pies are orange, so the spell technically worked.

"I need to be more specific," he said. He took the wand in his hand again and said, "Make me a pie that tastes like an orange... wait, what rhymes with orange?"

The wand gave a single sad spark and a wisp of smoke.

Whimsy sighed and blew a strand of brown hair out of his eyes. If his grandmother was still here, she would have known a word that rhymes with orange.

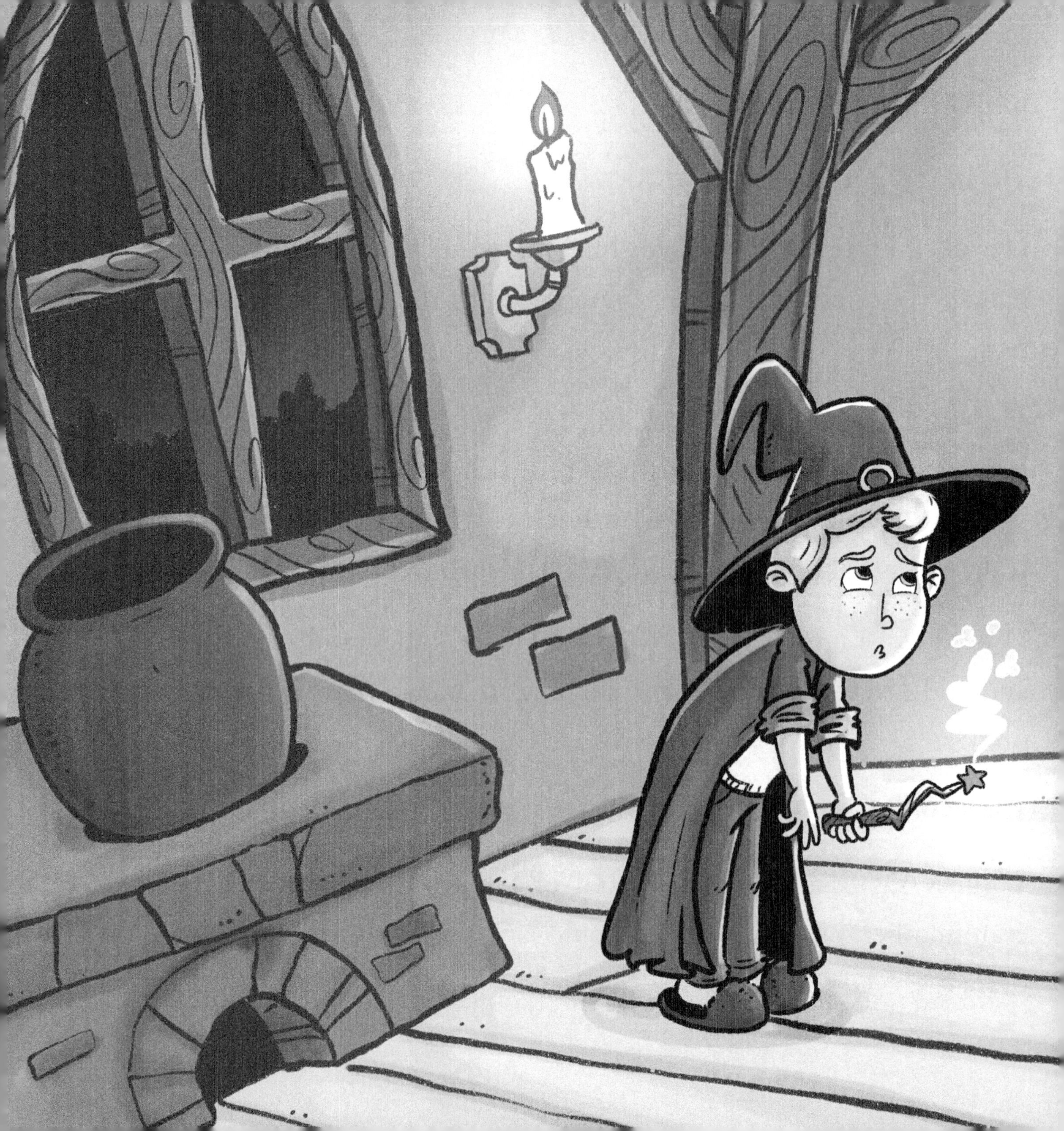

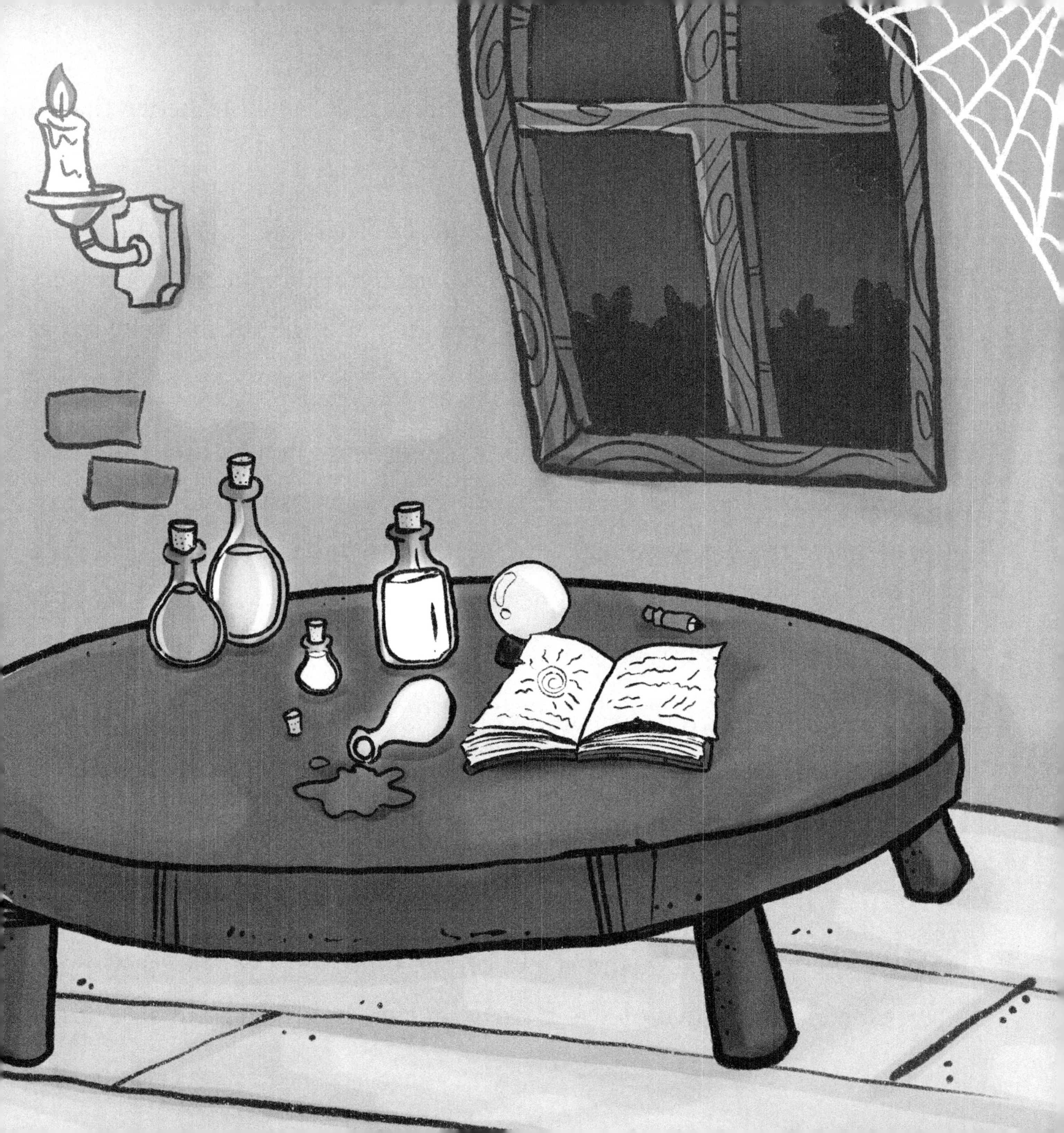

"Silly wand, I want pie with orange fruit, and make it taste better than a boot." He tried again.

The wand sparked and glowed and made another pie, pumpkin again. Whimsy was forced to admit it was an orange fruit. It did not taste very good this time. The wand had listened carefully, and the pie did taste better than a boot. Barely.

Whimsy left his house to go for a walk, which always helped him think. He passed the baker, who told him such a pie was not possible. He passed the house of Barty the Bat, who had traveled far and wide and never seen such a pie. No one Whimsy talked to knew how to make an orange pie. At least they were nice enough not to laugh at him.

Whimsy was determined. If he couldn't get the wand to make him an orange pie, maybe he could get it to make him every sort of pie ever created. Then he could go looking for the one he wanted. It was worth a try.

"This orange pie is on my mind, so give me pies of every kind!" he cried.

Suddenly, there were stacks and stacks of pie. One pie is delicious, two pies are even better, and three pies is a party, but every kind of pie all at once is entirely too much. There were blueberry pies and chicken pot pies and chocolate peanut butter pies. Pies were stacked to the skies.

Villagers rushed out of their homes, and pies spilled out when they opened the doors. They had to climb over pies to get to Whimsy. Some pies were hot and some were cold. Some were crispy, some were flaky, and some were soft. And they all squished together when the villagers climbed over them.

The first person to reach Whimsy was Bitey the Cat, who used to be a regular cat but had learned to talk just to cheer up her grumpy owner, Katey the Kitsune. It turned out that Katey was grumpy around everyone, and cheering her up was such a good idea that the villagers voted Bitey the Cat the mayor of Dewdrop Hill. It was an easy job, unless a wizard tried to make every kind of pie at once.

"Whimsy, that wand makes too much trouble! You have to take it out of Dewdrop Hill," said Bitey.

"But I like it so much!" Whimsy cried. "I can't bear to leave it. Plus, look at all the pie I made for everyone."

There was, indeed, a lot of pie for everyone. But it was on the ground, in the houses, in the stores, in the well. The pies were melting and crumbling and getting mashed together. People had to step on them just to come over and see what was happening. There were a lot of pies, but they were no good to eat.

"It will take us days to clean up this mess, and can you imagine how it's going to smell?" Bitey asked. "Pies are good in ovens and on plates and on windowsills. They are not good everywhere. I bet even the bathtubs are full of them! Please, please, please take the wand out of here, at least until you're more careful with it."

Other people had started to gather, and they did not look happy. They had pie on their clothes and in their hair and on their faces. It looked like the end of a giant food fight, but Whimsy was the only one playing—and the only one not covered in pie.

"I'll use the wand to clean it right up," Whimsy said. "It will only take a moment, if I can think of a rhyme."

"No!" everyone shouted.

And so Whimsy the Wizard left Dewdrop Village with his wand. He would be back soon, when everyone was in a better mood—probably after they finished cleaning up the sticky mess. But he still did not give up on his dream of a delicious orange pie.

He passed a bridge with a sign that said "Warning: Troll Toll Ahead" and gripped his wand tightly, because he had never met a troll before and he'd heard they were dangerous. But it looked like no one was home, so he continued on his way. Maybe his luck was changing.

Luck. That was it! Maybe he couldn't make an orange pie with his magic rhyming wand, but he might be able to make something else that could help him make his pie. Then he could go back to the village and show the villagers his delicious orange pie, and they would know he was getting better with his magic.

He pulled out the wand. He was nervous to use it again after the pie disaster, but he was determined.

"I want orange pie but you won't give me any, so instead give me a lucky penny!" said Whimsy.

The wand flashed and sparkled and smoked, and a tiny copper penny appeared in the air. Whimsy tried to catch it, but he missed. He picked it up off the ground. It was bright and shiny. Brand new. Was it really lucky? It looked like a normal penny, but Whimsy thought it felt lucky, at least.

But a lucky penny needed one more step.

"Is this thing lucky? I can't tell. Help me with a wishing well!" he said with a wave of the wand.

A big beam of light exploded from the wand—so big people could see it from far away. It was the most powerful spell Whimsy had ever used, but it worked.

In front of him was a beautiful stone well, gray with some marvelous green moss around it, and a sturdy wooden bucket was suspended over the well with a rope made of giant's hair. There was also a sign. It read: "The maker of this wishing well would like to wish you well." Whimsy liked that a lot. He wanted everyone to be happy.

"Perfect," Whimsy said.

He took the lucky penny in his hand, and he knew it would work just the way he wanted because it was lucky. Still, he wanted to be very clear.

"I would like an orange pie, please," he said. "A pie that tastes like oranges, and the most delicious pie I can imagine."

He tossed the lucky penny into the wishing well. It fell into the darkness and kept falling: way, way, way down, until there was a tiny splash.

"Hello there, friend!" called a voice behind him. Whimsy jumped, because a moment ago he had been alone on the path.

He turned and saw a large man with a large belly, dressed in white and wearing a tall white chef's hat. He was very clean, even though he should have been covered in dirt from the road. He had blue fur and whiskers, although Whimsy couldn't tell what sort of creature he was exactly. But more importantly than that, he had a cart of the most beautiful pies Whimsy had ever seen.

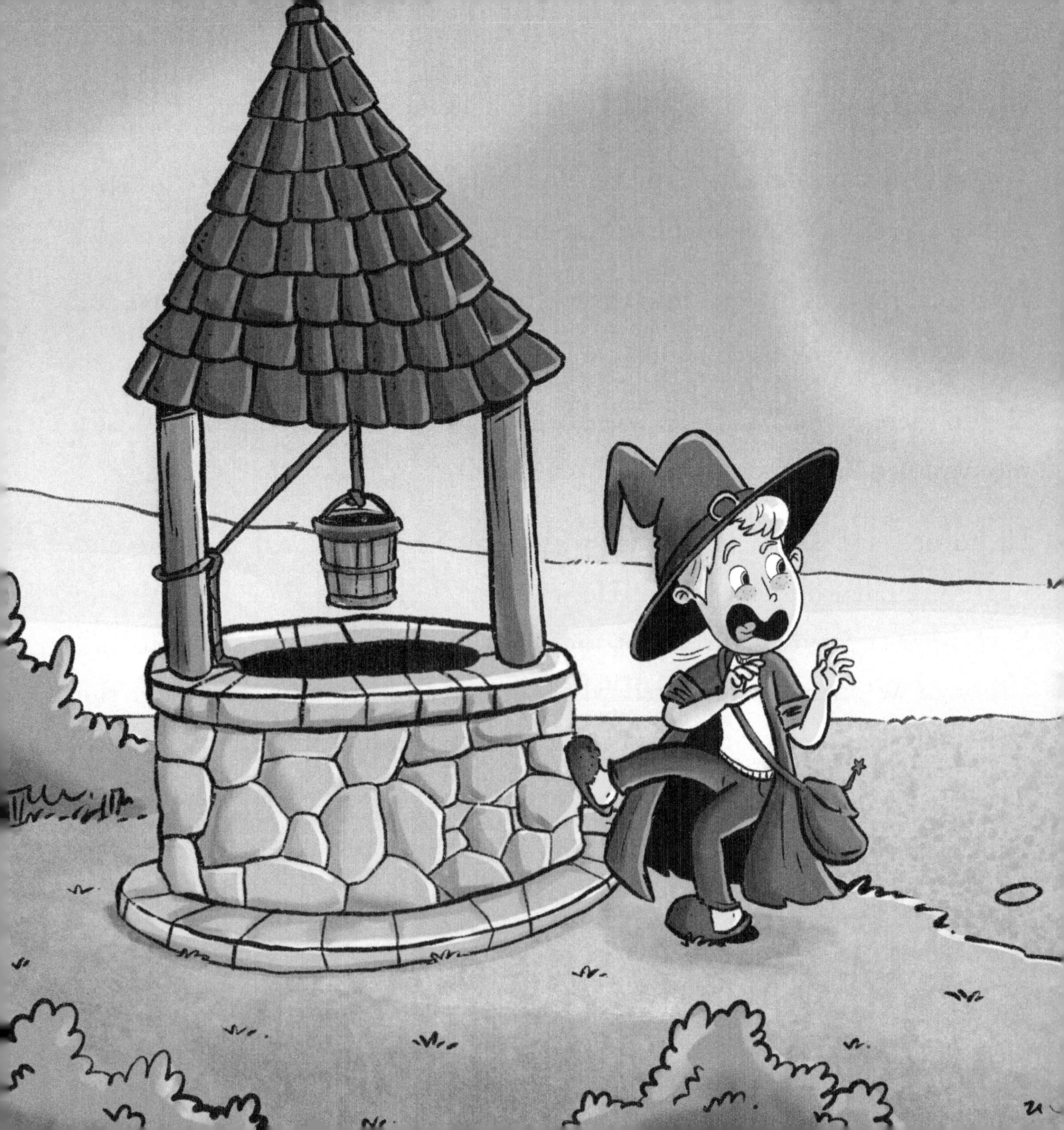

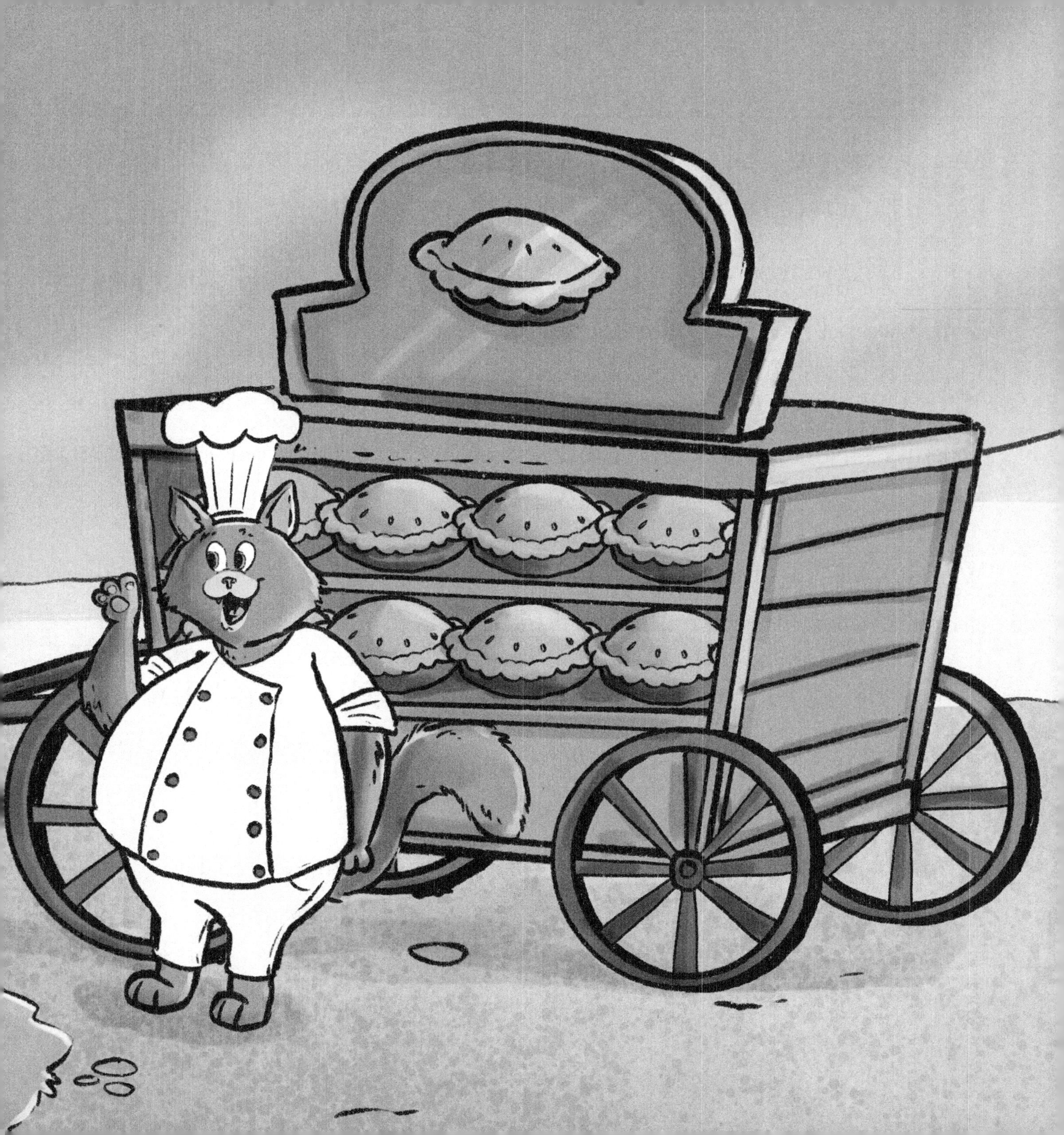

He walked over. The smell of the pies almost made him float. All of them were warm and fresh, although there wasn't an oven in sight. Apple pies, lime pies, mincemeat pies... and there, right in the center, an orange pie.

"Hello there," Whimsy said. "You have the most beautiful pies I have ever seen. I would like to try the orange pie very much."

"Oh, that one?" the baker said. He picked up the pie and handed it to Whimsy. "Most people think an orange pie is strange, but I think it's the best pie I ever made. You can have this one."

Whimsy was surprised. "Are you sure? I don't have any money, although I do have this wishing well, if you'd like to try it."

"That's okay," the baker said. "I have everything I need, so I don't need to wish for anything more. I suppose I wish people would try my delicious pies, but you can help me with that without a wishing well."

Whimsy jumped and did a little spin in his excitement. "Thank you so much! Are you sure there isn't anything I can do for you?"

The baker looked around, happy but confused. "Well, I don't really know where I am. I was at my bakery one moment, and then I was here. I don't know how, but I suppose it's where I needed to be! If you could point me to somewhere people would like my pies, I would be very happy."

Whimsy was embarrassed, but he wanted to be honest. "Dewdrop Hill is that way, and that's the way I'm going. But I don't think they'd enjoy your pie today. There was a bit of a magic mix-up, and I think they've had more than enough pie for one day."

The baker laughed a big loud laugh, and his whole big body shook. "I understand! We've all had a few pie-related disasters in our lives, right?"

He waved goodbye and pushed his cart down the road in search of more people to try his pies. Whimsy took his fresh orange pie back to Dewdrop Hill, so he could show them he was much better at magic than he had been that morning.

And that's the end of the story, because an unattended wishing well has never caused any trouble.

Franklin the Fairy Takes a Very Big Job

Franklin the fairy had been given his name at a very young age. He would like to try on some other names, but he didn't want to take them from anyone else, so he settled for being Franklin.

Franklin was very bad at school. Other fairies learned to be tricky and cunning, but Franklin would rather be honest and considerate. Other fairies learned to hide and watch, but Franklin was always curious and wanted to talk. Other fairies liked to play games and eat food, but Franklin liked painting and drawing. He knew he could be a very good… something, but he did not feel like a very good fairy.

One day, Franklin was playing alone, looking for something to be good at. Sometimes other fairies played with him and sometimes they didn't. He wished they would play with him more, but he was happy by himself, too. He was talking to a spider who was not interested in talking back to him, when suddenly, he heard a pop and a whistle and smelled some smoke. Then he found himself somewhere else altogether.

The inside of the cabin was neat and organized, except for a large bench with things scattered all about it. The only other person there was an old woman with long gray hair and a big, knobby cane. She was small for a wizardess, but she was still the biggest creature Franklin had ever seen. And she was looking right at him.

"Oh, you tiny little thing," she said. "I hope I'm not scaring you. I won't hurt you and I can put you right back in a moment."

"I never met anyone so big," Franklin said. "But I don't think you can hurt me, because I'm a fairy. I have a lot of magic, and you only have a little magic. I was talking to a spider, but she didn't say anything back to me, so I guess I'm talking to you now instead."

The wizardess smiled at Franklin's bravery, even though she had more than just a little magic. "I'm happy to talk with you," she said. "You can call me Grandma Wist, although I am keeping my name for myself."

"I'm Franklin! And I would like to keep my name, too. Actually, if you know someone who would like to trade maybe I would do that, but I don't want to be left without a name, and I don't think anyone else would like that either."

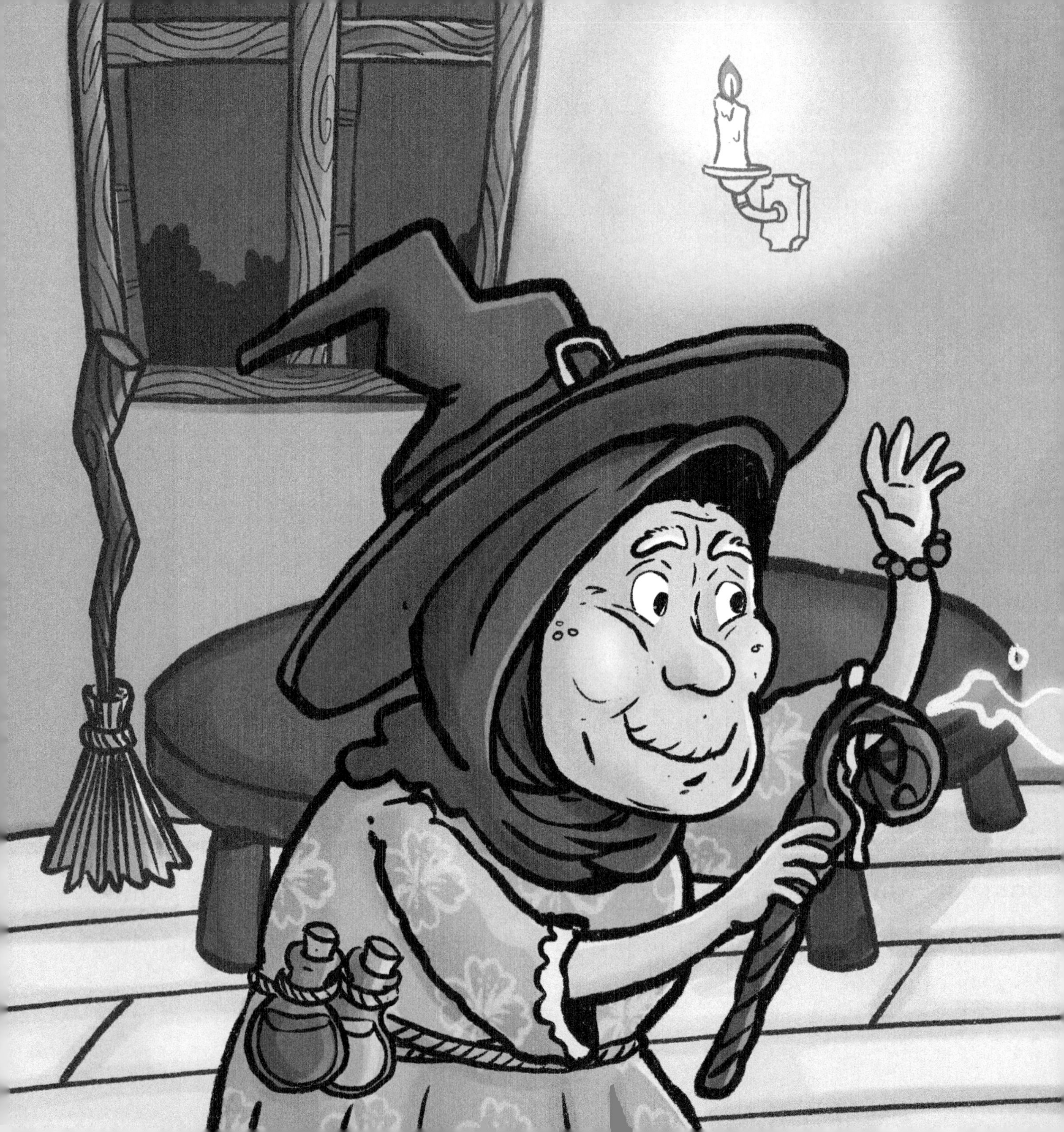

"If I meet someone who looks like a Franklin, I will let you know," Grandma Wist said. "And I'm terribly sorry for summoning you here without asking you first. But I need some help and I think you're just the right person for the job."

"I love to help!" said Franklin. It was very rare that other fairies wanted his help, so this seemed like a great opportunity.

"I need a fairy coin for a friend of mine in a faraway land. But you can't magic up a fairy coin out of nothing. A fairy has to give it to you."

"Oh, like this?" Franklin said.

He reached up with his small fingers, pinched at the air, and pulled. Then there was a fairy coin in his hand, simple as that.

"Here you go!" Franklin said, offering her the coin.

Grandma Wist was surprised. "I appreciate the coin very much, but perhaps before I take it we should talk about payment." Grandma Wist was very wise and knew she should not take anything from a fairy without offering something in return.

"I'm not really sure," Franklin said. "Perhaps I could give you the coin now, and when I think of something, I could ask you for help?"

"I like that idea," Grandma Wist said. "And I am thankful for your generosity. But I hope you can understand, it can be very dangerous for a wizard to owe a fairy a favor. Are you sure I can't pay you now?"

Franklin sat down on the wooden bench and thought carefully, because he knew wizards were very powerful. Some of them, anyway. He was worried that if he thought for too long the wizardess would get upset, but she was patient and kind. Eventually, he decided what he wanted.

"I feel like I'm very good at being me," Franklin said. "But I'm not sure I feel like a very good Franklin, or a very good fairy. Could I have a chance to try being something else?"

Grandma Wist clapped her hands in excitement. "Oh, I have just the thing. I have an old friend, very different from you, who wished for the same thing long ago. With a bit of magic, you could try to be him, and he could try to be you. Not forever, mind you. Just for a bit."

Franklin thought that sounded amazing. He could be himself, but something different, just for a little while. Then he could go back to being a fairy again.

"Deal," Franklin said. "You can make me something else, just for a while, and in exchange, I will pay you one fairy coin for your trouble."

"What a wonderful deal," Grandma Wist said. She reached out and gently took the fairy coin from Franklin. "I'm going to teach you a spell first. It's called a counterspell. It's the one you can use when you want to go back to being a fairy. It has to rhyme, or it won't work. You say 'I am me, whoever I be. In all the world I ever see, I can change as I like and always be me.' Can you remember that?"

Franklin repeated the spell to himself over and over, until he was sure he would not forget it. Even just thinking about the spell's words made him feel warm and happy inside.

"Got it!" Franklin said.

"Ready?" Grandma Wist asked.

"Ready!" Franklin said.

Suddenly, Franklin found himself floating in space. Well, not floating, exactly. His feet were standing on something, although he couldn't tell what. His feet also didn't feel like his feet. They were much larger and clunkier than his own tiny fairy feet.

"Wow," Franklin said.

There were stars all around him. Above him, below him, in front of him, and behind him. He was big and strong and old and everything he wasn't, when he was in his fairy body. It was hard to explain, but it filled him with relief. He knew his name was Naron for now, although he didn't know how he knew. And he knew the rock he was holding was the world, although he didn't know how he knew that either.

He held the world for a very long time. He was happy to be Naron the giant, because he was so big he could protect the whole world. It made him feel special and important, which were two things he had never felt before. But it still felt strange, because he wasn't himself. The world was starting to feel heavy, and he knew it was time to be Franklin again—but now he knew he could return, and find things that would make him feel special and important at home. He spoke the counterspell, which he still remembered even though it had been a very long time, because it was such a beautiful spell. "I am me, whoever I be. In all the world I ever see, I can change as I like and always be me."

And just like that, he was finished being Naron the giant, although he would always remember how good it felt to try something new. He was Franklin the fairy again.

Now he remembered what it was like to be a giant, very big and hairy and tired and full of ancient aches and pains. He still had a lot to learn about being a Franklin, but he decided then and there he would become the best Franklin the fairy realm had ever seen.

A Coin for a Wish

The treasure chest was easy to carry at first. Bobbles walked with care and he was strong and nimble, so he didn't mind the weight. He didn't have much use for the coins, but he did like the way they jingled.

But he had taken the coins from a dragon's cave and discovered the way he had entered the cave was too narrow for the chest. He found another way out, but it meant he would have to walk all the way around the mountain to get back to where he came from, and that was a long way to carry anything.

He hadn't gotten very far when he saw a band of knights riding horses. One of them was actually riding a large potbellied pig, but Bobbles didn't know if that knight was new or if he was the leader. He didn't know much about potbellied pigs, and he knew even less about knights.

"Ahoy there!" one of the knights said to Bobbles. Bobbles was pretty sure "ahoy" was something pirates said, not knights. But it was the first time he had ever met a knight, and he had never met a pirate, so maybe he was wrong.

"Ahoy?" Bobbles answered.

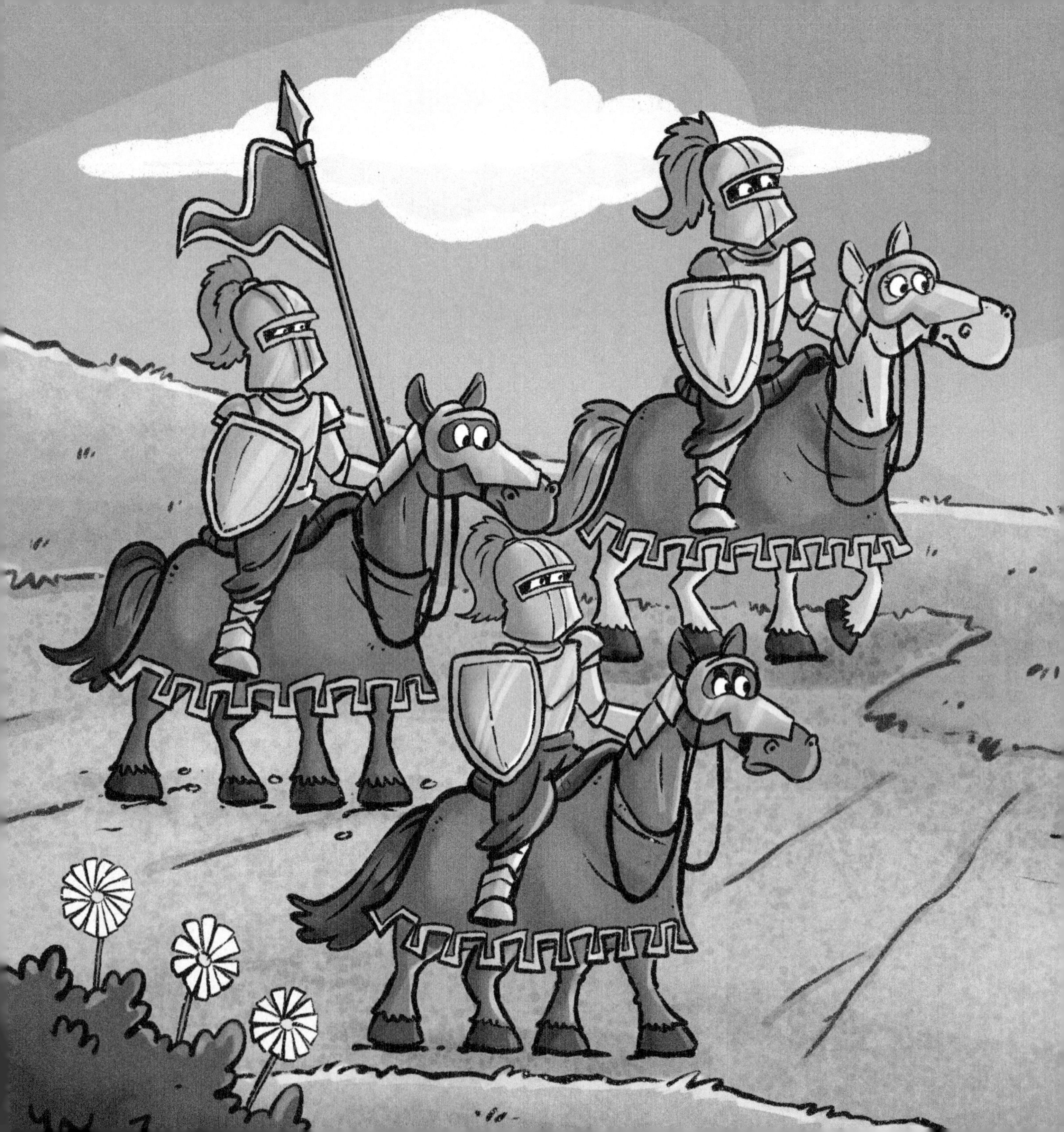

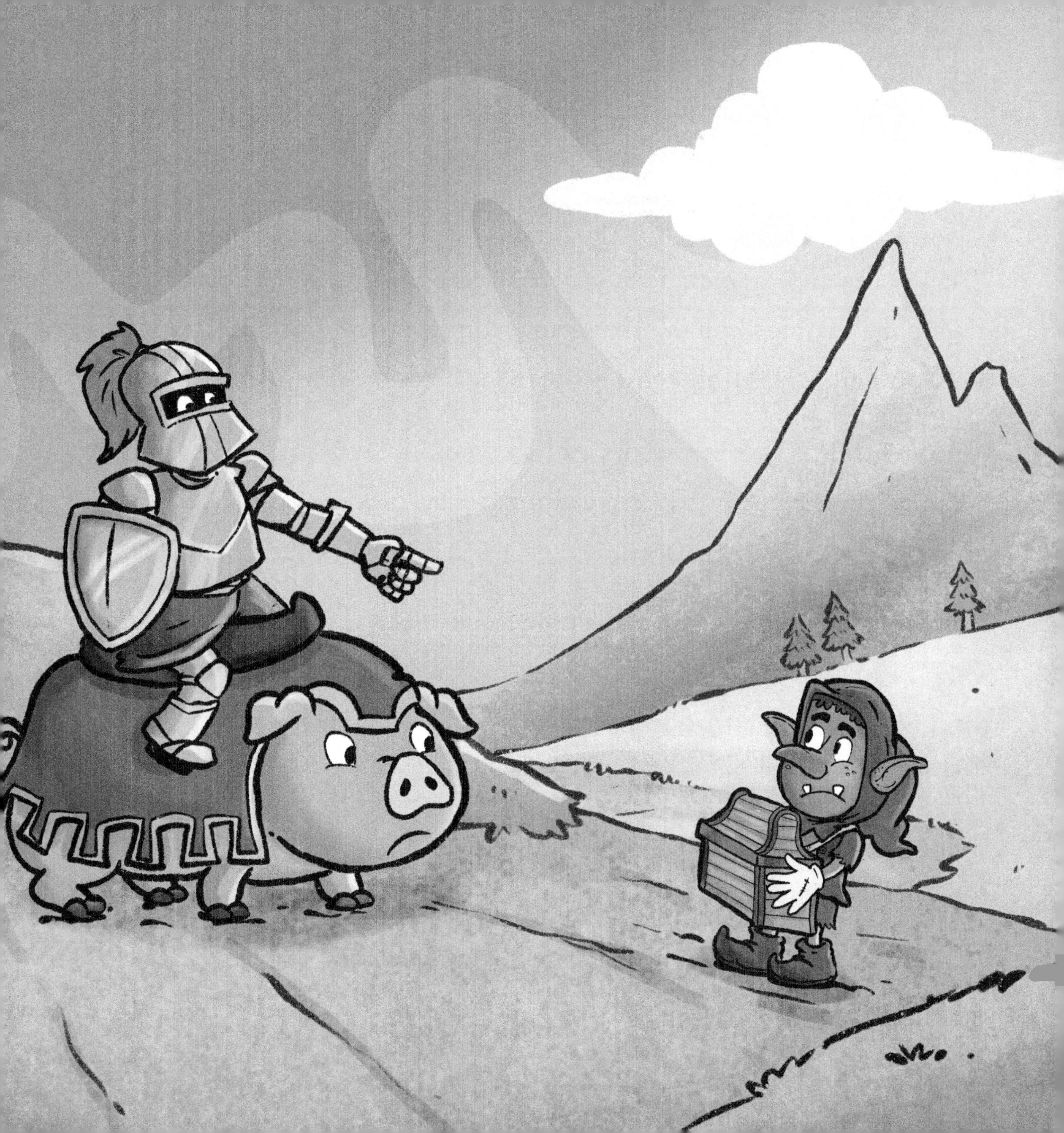

"Have you seen a great and terrible green dragon?" the knight asked. He had shining armor and a bushy beard, and was riding one of the horses. "We are supposed to slay the dragon and return with the treasure."

"I have seen the dragon, That's where I got this treasure! I don't think the dragon is terrible though. He seemed quite nice." Bobbles thought some more and added, "I don't think slaying is a good idea. Just in general."

"Terrible in this case means big and scary and dangerous," the knight on the pig corrected. He seemed very grumpy to be riding on a pig, and Bobbles decided he was not in charge.

"Oh," Bobbles said. "In that case the dragon is quite terrible indeed. If you want, I can give you some of the treasure I have with me. I have to keep some for a fairy queen, but I don't need all of it."

The knights talked among each other. It looked like they were arguing, but Bobbles couldn't hear them. He waited as patiently as he could. Eventually, the knights decided.

"For half your treasure, we will not slay the dragon," said the knight with the bushy beard.

The knights came closer and helped themselves to part of the treasure. Bobbles thought they took more than the half they promised, but he didn't mind.

"A gift from a goblin is better than being eaten by a dragon," one of the knights said.

They started to ride away, and Bobbles called after them. "You should say thank you you're not a dragon snack!"

The knights waved, and Bobbles went on his way.

He walked down a dusty path until he came to a river with a beautiful stone bridge across it. A troll sat under the bridge. He looked very tired.

"Hello there, mister troll! What's your name? Aren't you supposed to block the way and make me pay a toll or something?" asked Bobbles.

The tired troll got to his feet. "I suppose so. My name is Jammy, and I've just returned from a very long journey. I can make you pay the toll if you really want to."

Bobbles thought about it. "What are the tolls for, anyway? Do trolls need a lot of treasure?"

The troll climbed up from the muddy riverbed with great effort and did his best to brush himself off. "Who do you think fixes all these bridges? Without the toll, I could never get enough stone and brick and wood. A bridge could collapse and someone would get hurt."

"That sounds important," Bobbles said. "A bridge is really handy when you need one, and I wouldn't want anyone to get hurt."

Bobbles opened the treasure chest. He thought about all the bridges he had crossed in his life, and all the times he had wished for a bridge when there was none around. He dumped the coins out of the treasure chest. But he did want to bring some treasure to the fairies, so he picked up one of the coins and put it back in the treasure chest.

"That is very generous," the troll said. "That will help a lot."

"I think you need it more than me, so I'm happy to give it to you," Bobbles said. "Plus, now you won't have to worry for a bit, and you can take a nap."

Jammy thanked him several times, gathered the coins, and fell fast asleep.

The treasure chest was much lighter and easier to carry now, and Bobbles enjoyed his walk through the countryside. It was a bright and sunny day, and he would be back in the fairy kingdom soon. Soon, he came to a well, surrounded by beautiful, green, rather delicious-looking moss. There was a little boy sitting next to the well, and he looked sad even though it was such a nice day. Maybe Bobbles could cheer him up.

"Hi there, little boy," Bobbles said. " I've been walking for a very long time. Is it okay if I sit with you and take a rest? I promise I am not scary or dangerous."

"Of course you can," the boy said. "I know you're not scary. My grandpa is a goblin, although you can't really tell most of the time. I think some fairies switched him around when he was a baby."

Bobbles sat on the moss. In addition to being green and beautiful and delicious-looking, it was also quite comfortable. "I'm off to see some fairies myself, although I think I will be too busy to ask about your grandpa. My name is Bobbles."

"My name is Stormblast Thunderfist," the boy said. "I chose it myself!"

"Nice to meet you, Stormblast." Bobbles liked that name—goblins chose their own names too. "Can I ask why you're sad?"

Stormblast sighed. "I miss my friend. I live in Dewdrop Hill, but my friend had to move away. I found this well and I think it's magic, but the magic only works if you toss in a coin, and I don't have any. If I had a coin I could wish for my friend to come back."

Bobbles looked at the well and read the words on it. "The maker of this wishing well would like to wish you well." Then he looked at his treasure chest, with one single coin inside. He needed the coin to give to the fairies to save his brothers. Or, if he wanted, he could wish for anything he desired. But what he wanted most was to see his brothers again, and he was doing that already.

Bobbles opened up the treasure chest, and looked at the coin inside, silver and shiny. His last one.

"This is for you," Bobbles said. "I need this coin very much, but I think you need it even more, so I'd like to give it to you."

Stormblast jumped up in surprise. "I can have your very last coin? I don't have anything to give you."

"Yes, you do," Bobbles said. "If you see a chance to be helpful, you should do it. That will be the thing you can give to me."

Stormblast Thunderfist gave Bobbles a long hug, as tight and as strong as only someone named Stormblast Thunderfist could give. "Thank you so much," he said.

Bobbles gathered up his empty chest and they said their goodbyes. He carried the chest with him until he was back at the circle of mushrooms where his whole adventure had begun. He stepped inside and found himself back in the fairy realm.

He waited there, much more nervous than when he was in the fairy kingdom the last time, because he was alone. But he was excited too, because he would have his brothers soon.

Just like before, the fairies came to see who had entered their kingdom, carrying their bee-sting spears. Ana the fairy queen was with them.

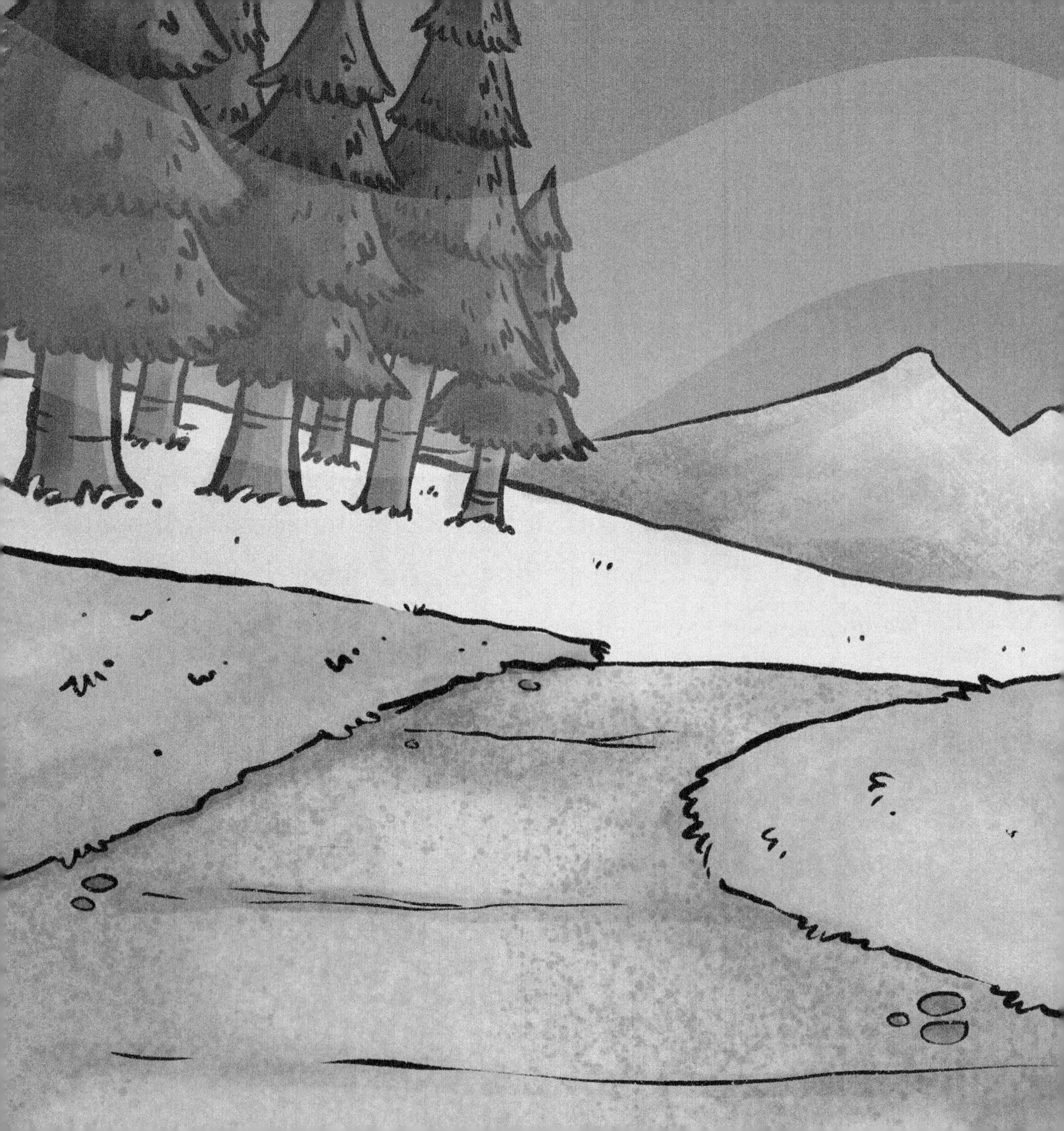

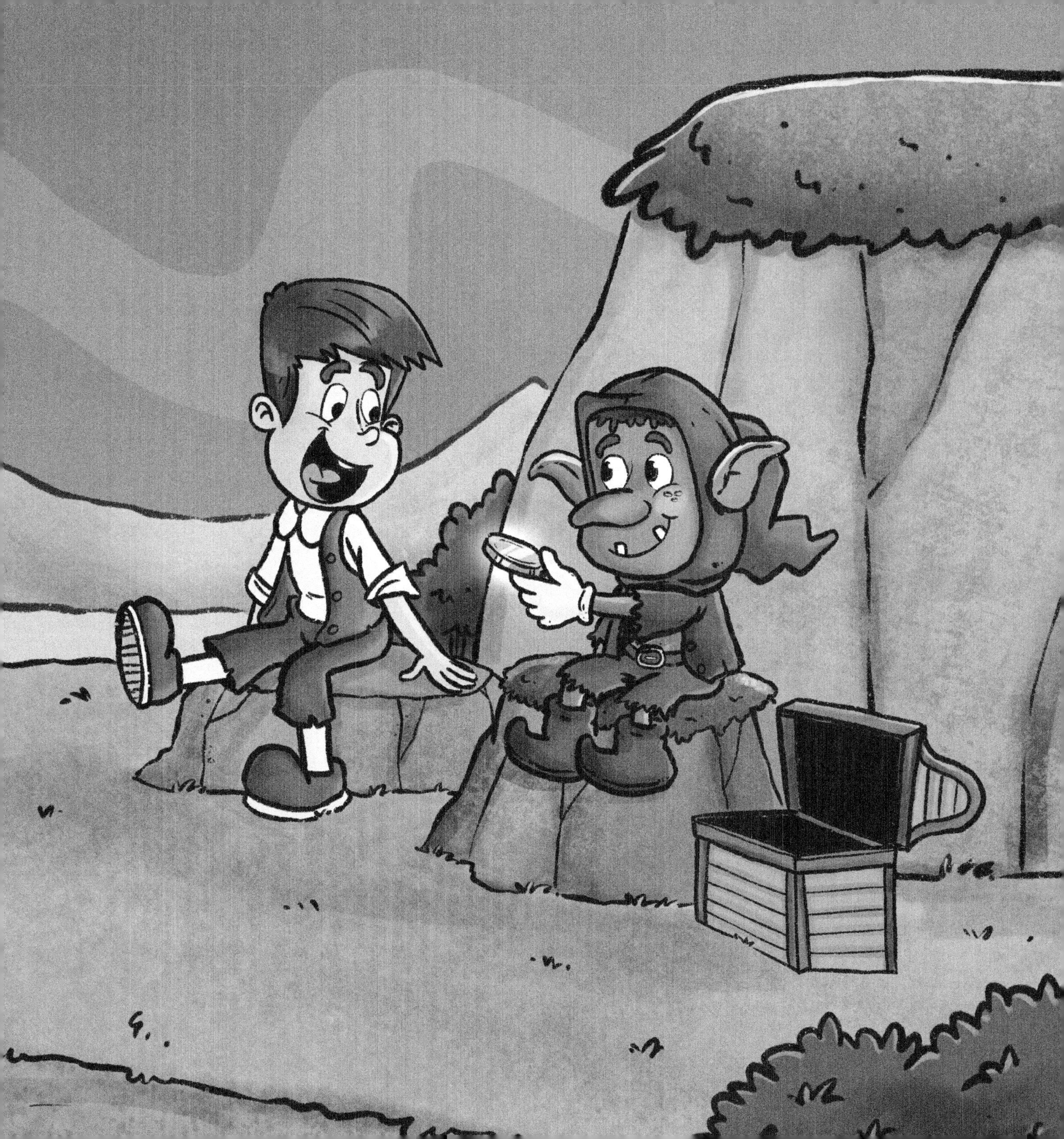

"Who goes there?" Queen Ana demanded. Then she looked closer. "Oh. It's you. Do you have my gem?"

"I did bring you something," Bobbles said. He held out the treasure chest.

She zipped up to the chest quick as a flash and used her magic to open the lid. She looked inside and saw that it was empty. Ana the fairy queen was not impressed.

"What is this?" she asked. "I'll tell you what this is. This is an outrage. Do you even want your brothers returned? You promised to bring back my gem!"

"I promised you I wouldn't come back empty-handed, and I kept my promise," Bobbles said.

"You are a foolish goblin," Queen Ana said. She was so angry she was shaking. "There's nothing inside. You didn't bring anything, promise-breaker!"

Bobbles held up a finger. "I did, though. I brought you this chest, straight from the dragon who has your gem. I brought it so you would know I talked to him, and I'm not lying to you."

Ana the fairy queen did not like being tricked. This wasn't a trick, exactly, but it felt like one.

"No Ear of the Fairy Queen, no brothers," Queen Ana declared. Behind her, the other fairies cheered in agreement.

"I would like to make a trade," Bobbles said. "I have an easy way for you to get your gem back, but I will only tell you if you let Bangles and my other brother come home with me right away. And you have to give my other brother his name back. I'm annoyed that I can't remember it."

Ana the fairy queen considered the proposal. She did not like being offered a deal. She liked to be the one offering the deals. But she wanted the Ear of the Fairy Queen very badly. "Tell me what you know and I will let your brothers go."

"And give my other brother his name back," Bobbles said.

"Ugh," Queen Ana said. "I will let your brothers go and give your other brother his name back. It didn't fit me very well anyway."

Bobbles told Queen Ana all about his adventures, because while different goblins liked different things, one thing every goblin liked was telling a story. He told her that she could trade the dragon his name in exchange for the jewel she wanted. He told her how brave he had been to face a terrifying dragon, and how he had been kind and generous to strangers. He left out the part about how he'd given away all the coins, but he was happy to have been so helpful.

At the end of the story, Queen Ana gave Bobbles his brothers, and Bobbles, Bangles, and Larry went home. It was a story they would tell again and again, every time they ate mushroom soup.

The Magical Meetup Mystery

Dewdrop Hill was in chaos. Three little goblins chased the mayor, Bitey the Cat, and the goblins in turn were chased by a large and smelly troll. Two small boys danced and played together in the town square, and an old woman sped after a young boy carrying a wand that sparked and smoked as he ran. At least half a dozen fairies flew about, casting spells on anyone who got too close and turning them into bats or pumpkins or very surprised fish. A dragon flew through the sky roaring and breathing fire into the air, while a knight riding a mud-covered pig shouted things at the dragon and waved his sword. And there was so, so, so much pie everywhere.

Katey the Kitsune was not from Dewdrop Hill, but she had lived there for a long time. She loved Dewdrop Hill, but the thing she loved most was solving mysteries. The people of Dewdrop Hill did not often need a magical, mystery-solving fox, but now was her time to shine. She shook her nine tails and looked around.

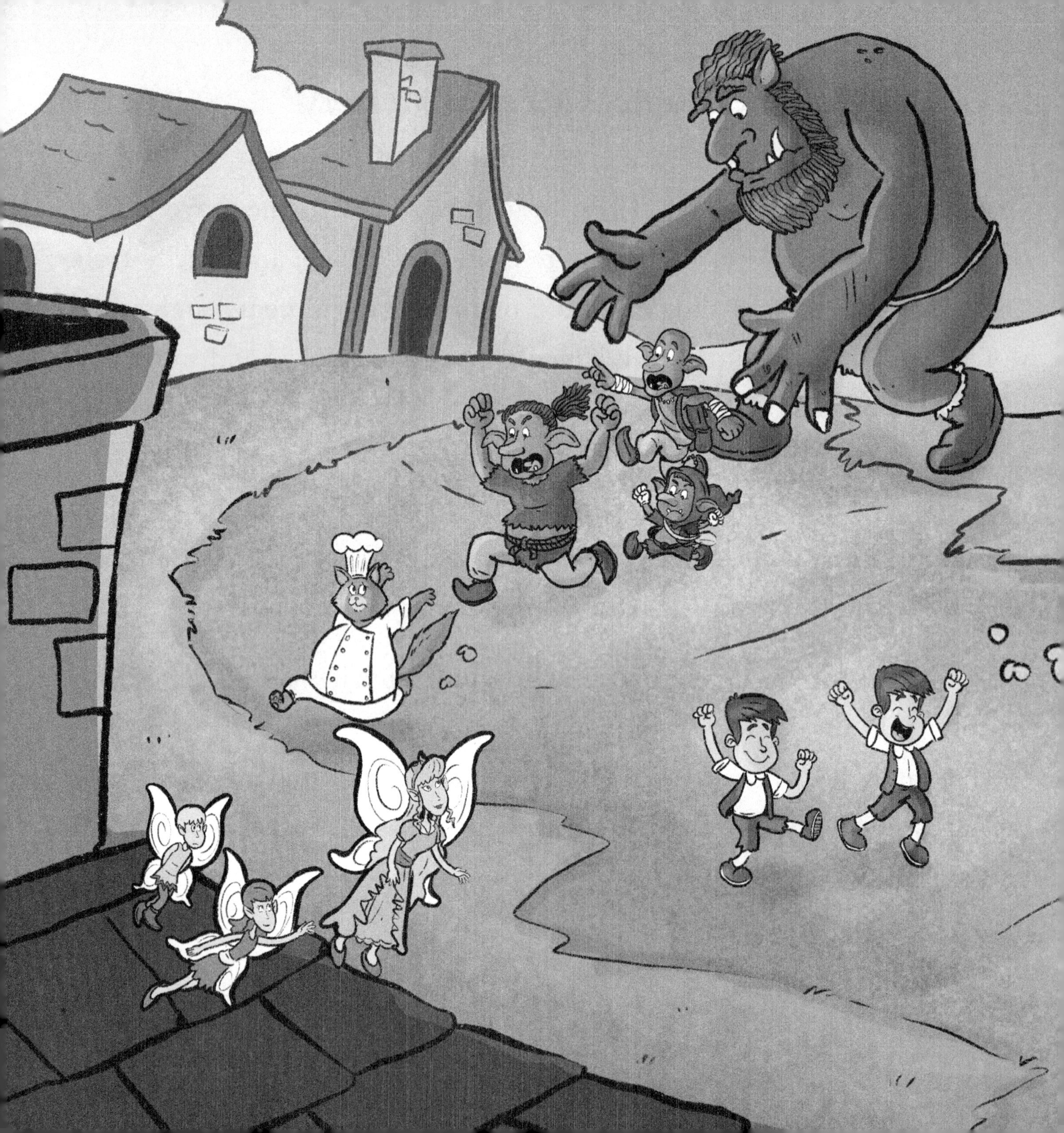

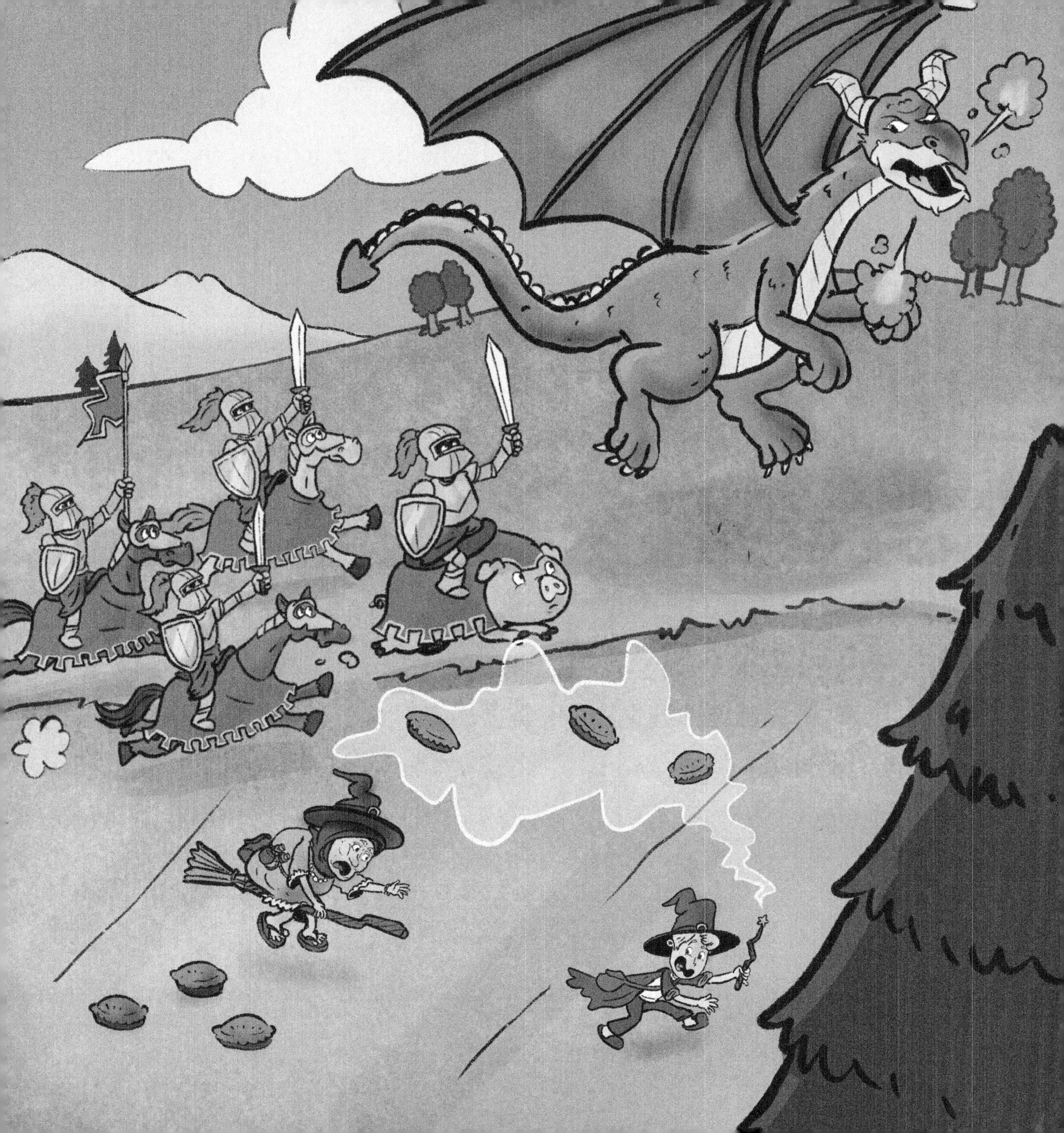

There were more people in Dewdrop Hill than she had ever seen, maybe more than had ever been there at once. If she didn't act fast, the whole place would be destroyed. But in order to act fast, she would have to act smart.

A knight—this one on a horse—raced toward her, and she jumped out of the way. "Excuse me, sir," she called after him as he galloped by. "But how did you get here?"

The knight was riding so fast he could barely answer her. "I don't know, but I've never seen a troll I couldn't defeat, and after I slay that one they will call me the mighty troll slayer!"

"Knights and slaying," Katey muttered. "They really need to cut it out." She looked at the mighty troll, who was chasing some laughing goblins. Katey doubted very much that the knight—even with a horse and a sword—would be doing any troll-slaying today. If there was one thing she'd learned by being a detective, it was that it was often better to act smart than to act fast.

"Young man!" an old woman shouted. Katey turned, even though she was not young or a man, and saw that the woman was talking to a little boy, who laughed and waved a magic wand that sparked and sizzled in protest. That,

Katey thought, was dangerous, even if it was very pretty.

A fairy flew by in a flash, so fast no normal creature could catch it. But Katey was as magical as they come, so she reached up and grabbed him easily and gave him a shake.

"What are you doing here?" Katey asked.

"I have no idea!" the fairy said. Behind him, a tower of pie crashed to the ground with a giant tumble and a squish. "We were bargaining with the dragon, and then the dragon was here, and so were we."

Katey let him go, and he zipped off. None of this made any sense, but now she had a lead. She considered her options and looked around for another way through the problem. For now, though, it seemed the dragon was the only choice.

She climbed to the top of her house, which was the biggest house in town now that her cat Bitey was the mayor and demanded extra rooms for all his toys and food dishes. She waved to the dragon high above her, who was still belching flames into the sky. The dragon flew down.

"Don't cook me," Katey called. "Why are you here?"

"I just want my name," the dragon said. "The fairies tricked me again. Bobbles the goblin left with my treasure, then the fairies came to see me, and now I'm here somehow!"

"They didn't trick you. They're just as confused as you are!" Katey yelled at him. Then she turned her attention to the goblins. She had another lead.

The goblins were running around, laughing as they ate pie after pie. They threw pies at each other and at other villagers, ignoring annoyed looks as they played. Katey grabbed the smallest one by the ear and gave him a shake.

"Where is the dragon's treasure?" Katey asked.

The goblin squealed in protest, but Katey didn't let go. "I gave some to the knights and some to the troll. I don't have it. I wanted to give it to the fairies so they would give me my brother's name back. Let me go so I can eat more pie!" The other goblins were gathering up as much pie as they could. When they couldn't carry any more in their arms, they went looking for carts to hold even more.

Katey looked at the knights, who were picking fights with the dragon or the troll or anyone else who got too close. The troll was busy chasing one of the goblins, who had hit him with a pie. Neither of them looked likely to be the cause of this.

"Who else?" Katey asked.

"I did give a coin to that boy over there," the goblin said.

In the middle of the town square, ignoring all the chaos around them, two young boys hugged and played, looking like long-lost best friends. Katey let the goblin go and approached the boys, who turned towards her as though they might be in trouble.

"I heard a goblin gave you a coin," Katey asked. "Can you tell me what you did with it?" She waved her tails for them, hoping it made her look friendly. Even with so much going on around her, Katey made sure she stayed calm.

"Hi, my name is Stormblast Thunderfist!" volunteered the boy the goblin had pointed to. "A very generous goblin gave me a coin to use in a wishing well."

Katey sighed. An unattended wishing well was a very dangerous thing, especially when it was found by little boys with coins.

"What did you wish for?" she asked.

"I wanted to wish for my friend to come back to Dewdrop Hill, but the goblin told me to do something nice for other people too, so I was going to wish for everyone's friends to come back. But then I thought I could make even more people happy, so I wished for everyone who wanted to visit Dewdrop Hill to be here, and it worked!" the boy said.

Katey let the boys keep playing. At least someone was happy. She wanted to run around helping all the confused people, but maybe, if she thought for a moment, she could find a better solution.

She spotted the old woman, who had given up chasing her grandson. Katey would take matters into her own paws. A little boy might be able to outrun his grandma, but not a magic fox. She grabbed the boy as he ran by, and snatched the wand from him.

"Unhand me, Miss Katey! I'm a wizard!" he cried.

Katey ignored him and took him over to his grandma. "I think this belongs to you," Katey said, handing the wand to the old woman. "I remember when you made that wand, long ago. It appears a fairy stole a goblin's name, someone used the wand to make a magic wishing well, and now literally everyone is in Dewdrop Hill. It's a rather long story."

"I can handle this," Grandma Wist said. She waved the wand and said, "This town is a wreck and a sight to see, put everything back how it used to be!"

The magic wand gave such a bright flash that everyone in town stopped to look at it. They watched as the mess cleaned itself up. The pies disappeared, and then one by one, the visitors disappeared too. Calm had returned.

"Oh, one more thing," Grandma Wist said with another wave of her wand. "A lovely boy is Stormblast Thunderfist, bring back his friend he likes the best."

"That's not a rhyme," Whimsy complained.

"It's my wand, and it does what I want," Grandma Wist said. "Now, let's go find a much calmer way to have some fun."

Thanks to Katey the Kitsune's careful and clever thinking, peace returned to Dewdrop Hill. Bobbles the goblin and his brothers lived happily in their forest home. Even though Bobbles was the smallest, Bangles and Larry always looked up to him since he had been so brave and wise and generous. No matter where their adventures brought them, their kind hearts, thoughtfulness, and perseverance helped everything work out in the end.

Leave Your Feedback on Amazon

Please think about leaving some feedback via a review on Amazon. It may only take a moment, but it really does mean the world for small authors like me 🙂

Even if you did not enjoy this title, please let me know the reason(s) in your review so that I can improve this title and serve you better.

From the Author

As a retired teacher, my mission with this series is to create premium inspirational content for children that will help them be strong in the body, mind, and spirit via important life lessons and inspirational messages.

Without you, however, this would not be possible, so I sincerely thank you for your purchase and for supporting my life's mission.

More titles you're sure to love!

Claim your free gifts!

(My way of saying thank you for your support)

Simply visit **haydenfoxmedia.com** to receive the following:

- 10 Powerful Dinner Conversations To Help Unlock Your Child's Potential

- 10 Magical Affirmations To Help Kids Become Unstoppable in Life

(you can also scan this QR code)

Printed in Great Britain
by Amazon